# CLOTH

# CLOTH

### A FATEFUL COMPROMISE WITH THE COTTON TRADE

Elizabeth Anderson

ISBN: 979-8-6703862-4-1

*In loving memory of my grandmother*

# CONTENTS

# ILLUSTRATIONS

# Introduction

WE HUMANS, AS OPPOSED TO ANIMALS, like our bodies to be covered up. Adam and Eve were said to sense their nakedness and feel the need to clothe themselves with fig leaves. It is impossible to know when people started making cloth because it is so perishable but flax fibers have been found recently that are 30,000 years old.[1]

So time-consuming is the preparation and spinning of bast fibers for weaving—flax, wool, hemp, cotton—and so universal the need for cloth, it is hardly surprising that cloth became the first mechanized commodity.

It is also not surprising that cotton became the particular kind of cloth that became industrialized. As late as the early nineteenth century, at least in northern Europe where only flax and hemp could be grown, clothing was very uncomfortable and hard to clean. When Europeans in their explorations of the globe discovered Indian handloomed cotton, its superiority was clear at once. It was soft and pliable and easy to clean and dye.

It was far from predictable, however, that the British would be the first Europeans to bring to market inexpensive cotton cloth rivalling the quality of Indian cottons. The more likely candidate would have been the Portuguese or Dutch, who had earlier global empires and had already exported Africans to work as slaves in sugar plantations in South America. But by the mid-1600s Portugal was in decline and the Netherlands was pursuing the spice trade leaving Britain free reign with the Indian cloth trade.

The cotton mills in Glasgow and Manchester, produced the first cheap cotton cloth in the 1780s. The product was the culmination of two centuries of experimentation in speeding up spinning with a series of domestic inventions, and in refining the quality of the thread—largely accomplished by raiding Indian weaving workshops and replacing Indian middlemen with British merchants— all under the watchful eye of the fearsome British East India Company. Founded in 1599 as a joint stock company to enrich its investors, the Company also had the power, by royal decree, to wage war and expropriate land as though it were a nation-state.

This extension of British power in the East was accompanied by territorial expropriation in the Western hemisphere: land along the east coast of North America stolen from indigenous peoples; and from other European powers, the war trophies of Guyana in South America, and islands in the West Indies.

From an unpromising start Britain had won possession of the prerequisites for dominating every aspect of the cotton industry: the slave labor of growers from African colonies; tropical island colonies in the Caribbean where the *Gosyppeum* seed could be grown; the cheap labor of British mill workers; a global empire of markets; and merchant-traders like John Grant to search for new markets and extend the bounds of the empire. The British had integrated four continents into an efficient "machine" for producing and selling cotton cloth, each with its specific contribution.

Brute force and ruthlessness were necessary to keep each link functioning in the chain for if one failed the whole system failed. If a rebellion of slaves or mill workers was not contained by whip or gun, or if markets were blockaded in war by a belligerent nation stopping exports of cloth and imports of raw cotton, mills would be shuttered, mill workers laid off, merchants and governments bankrupted.

By concentrating efforts on the production of cotton cloth and largely abandoning domestic farming, Britain became dependent on North America for food. This would cause famine later for John Grant's parents and family in Scotland when imports from North America were prohibited during the French wars.

Those who owned the means of production and received the profits from increased production were the capitalists—factory owners and investors. Their powerful ally, the British government, shared in the profits.

In its heyday, British factory owners, investors and the government collaborated in a vastly profitable enterprise which was grounded in exploitation of largely people of color and expropriation of land from indigenous peoples, causing incalculable suffering. The elements would remain the same in succeeding centuries, but combinations and geographic locations would change. "Constant shifting and recombination" is the very essence of capitalism, writes Sven Beckert, "Capitalism both demands and creates a state of permanent revolution." Its constant regrouping is only possible because of the "existence of places and people whose lives can be turned upside down." [2]

This is the story of John Grant and his family and how capitalism turned their lives upside down in the first century of the Industrial Age.

# 1

## THE DISTAFF AND SPINDLE

BEFORE JOHN GRANT'S FATHER, Alexander, left in the morning to teach his class at the charity school, he reminded his son to get busy taking care of the peats. Peat was the only fuel left for heating. Trees had been cut down centuries before. John, twelve, the eldest child, needed no reminders, but he was respectful in his reply for he admired and loved his father. In the short northern summers, he knew to start every day digging in the peat bogs. He was careful to cut the strips straight and to layer them so rain would run off and not puddle. The peats had to be completely dry to make a fire. In a few weeks, he would load the slabs onto a sledge and haul them back to the cottage. It would take seven or eight loads of the sledge. With the last strip cut for that day, he slung his heavy shovel to his shoulders and inspected the pile. Almost enough to get through the cold season, he estimated.

When John had left to cut the peats, Janet, his stepmother, was sitting at the spinning wheel, and when he returned he was not surprised to see her still sitting at the wheel with Anne, four, and Catherine, one, still playing at her feet. Their mother had given them a basket to play with filled with soft tow, pale yellow-colored flax too coarse to weave. Spinning took up all her time, except for preparing meals, doing dairy tasks or caring for her younger children. It took seven times longer than weaving. But it took less time with the wheel than with the distaff and spindle she had used when she was younger She spun and wove all the clothes, sheeting and diapers for the family. The spinning was unending, as babies were born, children grew and clothes wore out. Nevertheless, John remembered that, as a young child, she had dropped her spinning and weaving at a moment's notice when he needed her, for in later years he called her "my indulgent mother." Catherine had fond memories of her mother spinning. She had watched her carefully, trying to copy her— for it was a slowly acquired skill—and she had become a spinning teacher when she grew up.

*The Spindle (left) and Distaff (right).*
*Spinning tools used from ancient times into the nineteenth century.*

Of John's siblings only William, seven, was old enough to help him with growing and preparing the flax for spinning. The gap in their ages wasn't too big for a little teasing when they got down to the bog to check on the flax. John splashed William surprising him and William splashed him back until they were both soaked and their skin stained from the red-brown water. At last, with a few pokes of the bundles, they decided they weren't soft enough to take out yet. The long process had begun with planting the flax seeds in spring and harvesting the plants in late summer. After combing the seeds from the flower heads for planting next spring they'd tied the stalks into bundles and laid them in the bog to soften. When they were finally ready, they'd untie them and spread the loose stalks on the grass to dry. Breaking, scutching and heckling followed. These processes loosened the stalks' outer covering from the thin inner fibers their mother would spin.[1] She would lay all the fine fibers, just eighteen inches long, on the ground parallel to one another and roll them on to her distaff. Flax made a coarse linen used for all the family's clothing.

The Grants' parish minister said the women were a model of industry. But he chided the men—surely not Alexander— for being stubborn, lazy and backward, "satisfied with following the mode [of cultivation] used by their grand-sires," instead of adopting modern English methods. Nor did they produce anything to be exported such as yarn as some parishes did. "No article is manufactured for exportation" except "the distilling of Aquavitae." Unfortunately, the parishioners consumed it before it could be exported. Without industry, "the people are idle for a considerable part of the year."[2]

One fire heated the single-room cottage. The musky smell of the peat burning constantly on the hearth permeated the small space. Tall box beds divided the "ben," the sleeping end of the single room from the "but," the kitchen end. As a very young child, John had slept with his mother in a box bed of pine, concealed in the end wall of the kitchen, the door kept open toward the fire. On winter nights the few cattle, sheep and goats the family owned were led into the barn attached to the cottage, to be warmed by the same fire that heated the family. In the kitchen end of the room, a cupboard held their pewter dishes and the remainder of their few possessions. A kettle rested on a grate, and a three-legged pot stood on the hearth. When the family found a rare moment to rest, Alexander sat in the only chair, while John, his mother and siblings used low stools called creepies. There was no table.[3]

Alexander was a teacher for the Scottish Society for Propagation of Christian Knowledge (SSPCK). The Society was founded in Edinburgh in 1709 to convert Episcopal and Catholic Gaels in North Britain to the Presbyterian Church, and to teach them English so they could read the Bible.[4]

The examinations of potential teachers were conducted exclusively in the lowland city of Edinburgh, obliging Highland applicants to walk as far as 150 miles. The interview lasted several days and tested their Gaelic and English literacy, knowledge of arithmetic and literature, and, above all, their loyalty to the Presbyterian Church and English Hanoverian monarchy. "Only persons of Piety, Loyalty, Prudence, Gravity, competent knowledge [of] literature and imbued with other Christian qualifications suited to that station"[5] need apply. The SSPCK found few qualified applicants so they asked parish ministers to suggest candidates. The Rosskeen minister had watched Alexander grow up and had seen he was a bright boy. Indeed he was already assisting at a parish school in Tollie. So the SSPCK called on Alexander and he walked to Edinburgh to be examined. Of those who passed the exam, some were later dismissed for such things as trying to make money on the side or going fishing. And many quit. But Alexander, appointed to a school in Rosskeen parish at sixteen, would serve fifty-three years, ending only with his death.[6]

The landlords of the parish were required to provide houses, vegetable plots, schoolhouses, barley and a small salary for the masters, which they did with parsimony and only under duress. Judging from a drawing of one schoolmaster's single-room cottage, Alexander's may have been about twenty-five by twelve feet. One schoolmaster and his family were given a sheep house, the roof too low for anyone to stand up. Alexander was fortunate to receive a salary in addition to a house and barley though the salary of £12 a year didn't go very far.[7]

When Alexander was elected Secretary to the Presbytery Court, or Session, an honor for one so young, Sir John Gordon, the only landlord living in the parish, was angry that his candidate for the position lost five to two. He made Alexander's life difficult during his term and at first refused to give him a recommendation when he was appointed to a Society school in the parish of Urray. When he finally relented the Session wrote the necessary letter to the SSPCK.

*These certifie that the Bearer hereof Alexander Grant, a married man, lived in this Parish of Rosskeen for the space of sixteen years past, teaching the Charity School at Strathreesdale, until by appointment of the Society for Propagating Christian Knowledge, he was removed from it to the Parish of Urray about the 28th June 1774, and that he was a Communicant [permitted to take communion] for several years back, during all of which time, he behaved himself soberly and inoffensively, giving very great attention and appreciation to his Charge as Schoolmaster, and free from any Scandal or Church Censure or anything unbecoming his station or profession so that there is nothing known to us, to hinder his reception into any Christian Society or Congregation where Providence may order his lott. Given in Name and by appointment of this Session of Rosskeen on this 19th day of June 1775 years, and subscribed by.[8]*

The SSPCK teachers were required to speak only English to children who only understood Gaelic. Eventually the organization dropped the rule, and even commissioned a Gaelic translation of the Bible. Their purpose after all, was to teach the Highlanders to read the Bible, to make them Presbyterians.

This "cultural colonialism," by the SSCK of the Highlands, as Margaret Szasz calls it[9] became more relentless after Gaelic Scots risked all in what would be a final rebellion against the English in a long history of rebellions. The Rising, as it was called, culminated in a bloody battle at Culloden, near Inverness in 1746. Alexander would have been born about then. If his father had joined the losing rebel-side  it might explain why Alexander, his son, was a poor tenant, yet spoke English and was well educated, unlike most Highlander.

The battle of Culloden was an event of "extreme importance in the history of the town," an Inverness historian and current resident wrote in 2004, "and is still important in how it sees itself." The English supporters of the Hanoverian King won, but even fresh from victory, they were still thirsting for blood. One followed unarmed men into a house and "hashed them with his broadsword to death." In another incident, a woman, just widowed from the battle, came home to find sixteen dead men in her house only to be accused by the English as a "'rebel bitch,' otherwise why would so many wounded have sought succour at her door." They shot her tenant and his son and a beggar woman spinning in another house. Others who had taken no part in the battle and had taken refuge in Culloden house were dragged out and shot.[10] All this carnage, though the victims were not supporters of Charles Stewart, the Catholic Pretender to the throne and the supporters of the Protestant King George II had already won the battle.

The Protestant townsmen of Inverness had not been, by and large, partial to the leader of the revolt, except the Fraser clan and its chief, Simon Fraser, Lord Lovat. Yet the English had dealt with Inverness residents as savagely as if they had been rebels. "We are all accounted Rebells," one of the burghers lamented to a friend afterward. "We have no persons to complain to, nor do we expect redress."[11] Even two years later, the magistrate of the town recalled the infamous day with fresh pain: "I do not think there were ever greater inhuman barbaritys and cruelties of all kinds, perpetrated in anie countrie."[12] The English had nearly leveled the burgh. "The town appeared little better than the ruins of what it formerly was," the ministers of Inverness wrote. "In the centre of the town there were many ruinous houses, and in all the other parts of it, every second space, and that by far the larger, exhibited the ruin of a kiln, a granary or other building."[13]

After the battle, the English arrested Simon Fraser Lord Lovat, took him to London and beheaded him. Frasers in general bore the brunt of the punishment from the English and many Frasers emigrated. The lands belonging to the rebelling clans were forfeited to the English, and everyone was forbidden to wear the plaids, to play bagpipes or to participate in any of the other ancient clan-related practices and duties. And, for good measure, the SSPCK stepped up its activities— which is about the time Alexander was hired as a teacher.

Twenty-four years after the Rising, in February 1769, John Grant was born to Alexander Grant and Christian McKenzie in Rosskeen parish.[14] John was five when his father was transferred to the Society school in the parish of Urray, and he grew up there. Lord Mackenzie of Seaforth, as all landlords were required, provided a cottage and vegetable plot for Alexander's family on his estate of Fairburn, one of several estates he owned in Scotland.[15] Seaforth derived his wealth from his Jamaican cotton plantation.

By age ten, John began an apprenticeship in nearby Inverness with a cloth merchant. His father felt that there was no future anymore for a Highland boy in Scotland. He arranged an apprenticeship for John with the help of an old friend, Alexander Fraser, a former SSPCK teacher turned merchant. By then Inverness was very prosperous-looking compared to the hardscrabble farms in Urray. It was a clear demonstration to the boy of the rapid pace of economic change, and of the promising future of merchants. Since the Rising there had been "a great influx of money from the

East and West Indies into the burgh" —from sugar plantations in the Caribbean, cotton from India, and tobacco from the Upper South of pre-revolutionary America.[16]  By consenting to a union with England in 1707, all the colonies of Britain had been opened up to Scottish merchants and they had jumped at the opportunity, going out to the East or West Indies. The new wealth of these merchants was plain to see in the town. The successful plantation owners in the West Indies lavished gifts on their hometown—a new academy, the Northern Infirmary, and a handsome building for the Northern Meeting (a new social club for the gentry). They were much admired by the ministers for these gifts and for their extensive gardens and other improvements to their estates.[17] Less well known was the barbaric treatment of the slaves.

Exposed to such affluence, many young people, including some of John's relatives and friends, craved the same luxuries and went out to the West Indies. As one Scot planter observed, "I am astonished, that any Person can think of In[j]uring there children so much Who are not born to Independent fortunes, as compleat and in such a miserable country when they have such a Country as Grenada, St. Vincent or the other West Indea islands to send them to, or what do you think of the East Indies for a change?"[18]

Since the 1740s Scottish merchants had depended on slave labor in the West Indies and had transported millions from Bance Island, a British colony on the west coast of Africa, to their sugar plantations in the Caribbean. Some made immense fortunes from the free labor of the African slaves and the free islands from the British Empire.

But not everyone who went to the West Indies would be successful. Disease, slave revolts, bad markets, wars, crop failures, the rigors of the climate and the dangers of ocean travel would kill many of them first. One planter wrote home that there was little need for him to send frequent letters because every day brought "a train of disappointment."[19] Another planter wrote: "You may be sure I have the utmost anxiety to bid this part of the world adieu," with its hell-ish climate. [20]

One visitor called the islands "a vortex of dissipation."[21] Miscege-nation occurred across all social classes, from plantation owners to the lowest classes of whites, and soon many mulatto children with Scot-tish names like Angus, Duncan and Malcolm peopled the islands of the West Indies, most adding to the slave population. Some fortunate few were sent to Britain or America for an education; others were freed and became wives of their owners or slave owners themselves.

Only the constant threat of brutal punishment for the most insig-nificant infraction kept the outnumbered white owners in power. Perhaps, tragically, the Scots in the West Indies, who were largely Fraser Highlanders, passed on to their slaves the abuse and mistreat-ment they had suffered at the hands of the English in the Rising of 1745-6, and perhaps it was their guilt that induced them to build so many churches there.

Those who became wealthy from their West Indian estates, managed by others or recently returned themselves, slipped into debt from overspending on newly available luxuries. Lord Seaforth was one of them and considered selling his estate of Fairburn. The indebted landlords often looked to their land as a way to get solvent, evicting tenants who paid rent in barley and meal and replacing them with sheep that could be raised more inexpensively and whose wool could be sold for cash. For a while the Grants had been nervous about not being able to stay on Fairburn but fortunately Seaforth decided not to sell. The Clearances, as the removal of tenant farmers came to be known, forced hundreds of thousands of Scots to emigrate.

During this tumultuous time John went to a counting house in London, the usual education for a merchant, and either before or after, served in an English regiment in the two-decade-long French wars. On returning to Scotland, he married a Miss Frazier in Inverness in 1801. Four children were born to them, three in

Inverness. The first, Mary Fraser, was born in 1802.[22] The second, Simon Fraser, named in memory of the still beloved Fraser leader, Lord Lovat, died as an infant. The third, Alexander Fraser, was born in 1805.[23] After their son's birth they moved to Glasgow where Hectorina was born in 1807.[24]

Glasgow was a busy port on the Atlantic. In the early to mid-1700s its merchants had grown wealthy importing tobacco from pre-revolutionary America and sugar from slave plantations in the West Indies. The city also had a thriving export business in hand-loomed fine linens, silk gauze and fustians (cotton with a linen warp). A kind of proto-capitalism had developed in the cloth trade, consisting of merchants buying or offering credit to female home spinners in a "putting out system," then giving the yarn to workrooms of six or so male weavers, and finally selling the finished pieces in distant markets. Through this experience, merchants had developed shipping methods and sophisticated financial tools for importing and exporting goods over long distances— bills of exchange, extension of credit, marine insurance. and the like.

In the 1780s, Glasgow experienced an influx of raw cotton from Scottish-owned Caribbean plantations. Men with scientific and mechanical skills, who had accumulated capital from trade in the early 1700s, or had obtained it through kinship or marriage, built mills to spin the raw cotton. Spinning had always been the bottleneck in the cloth-making business. These early mills used water power from streams outside the city. Construction began in 1778[25] and by 1812, there were 120 spinning mills around Glasgow.[26] Their spinning machines— James Hargreave's jenny improved by Richard Arkwright and Samuel Crompton— were able to spin cotton thread strong enough to replace linen warps, enabling mills for the first time to produce fine cottons and muslins to rival India's.

Scottish mills also excelled in cloth's finishing trades. Using artists' knowledge of printing with copper plates on paper, and scientists' experiments with bleaches and dyes, mechanical engineers invented roller printers, capable of producing thousands of yards of calico a day, matching the quality of India's calicoes and far exceeding its productive capabilities.

The mills employed young children and women who worked twelve to fourteen hour days for subsistence wages or none at all. The population of migrants from the Highlands and Ireland flocking to the city exceeded the city's ability to employ, house or feed them; they lived in squalid conditions in alleyways where diseases spread easily. A few paternalistic mill owners like David Dale provided shelter and food for his workers.

John Grant was interested in touring all the mills, seeing and feeling the different kinds of textiles available, hearing how they were made and meeting the managers and owners. He surely visited the most successful cotton mill in Glasgow, New Lanark Mills. Welshman Robert Owen, part-owner, manager and son-in-law of David Dale, had increased the company's profits by fifteen percent in the early 1800s and later by forty-six percent.[27] His success attracted many curious visitors.

One of these was Robert Southey who described his 1819 visit to Owen's mill in an article he titled "Utopia." The mill workers were mostly paupers, many of them evicted Highlanders. Owen housed them in clean apartments and paid for their medical care. Most ingenious on Owen's part was his promise to educate the children in exchange for reduced wages for the parents. Owen amassed a fortune. However, by the time of Southey's visit, Owen had become more interested in what he called "The Formation of Character" than in profit-making, and was building concert and lecture halls out of his own funds.

For Southey's visit, Owen had planned a performance of two hundred children dancing, marching and piping. Southey noted how much Owen and the children enjoyed this, boring as it was to him for the children acted like puppets. Indeed, Owen referred to the children as "human machines." The children seemed to Southey to differ from slaves on cotton plantations only in color. Owen "keeps out of sight from others and perhaps from himself, that his system instead of aiming at perfect freedom can only be kept in power by absolute power."[28] On the other hand, another visitor, William Maclure, a Philadelphia educator, was thrilled to see the factory children in school and didn't remark on any puppet-like movements.

In 1825, to try out his theories, Owen sold his ownership share in New Lanark Mills and with the financial help of William Maclure purchased George Rapp's town of Harmonie in Indiana. The town, which Owen named New Harmony, would figure prominently in the lives of some of the Grant children who attended the school founded by Maclure, or contributed work for the general good of the community. While the socialist experiment failed after two years, the school was a success and continued after Owen left. Owen died penniless having used up all his money funding New Harmony and others like it. None lasted more than a few years but his theories inspired socialists. Owen passionately believed that with the proper training, people could be purged of their desire for individual property and liberated from the deceptions of religion. (It was rumored that Owen had grown up surrounded by a particularly pernicious form of Calvinism.)

In 1806-7, cotton mill owners in Glasgow suffered grave losses shortly after Napoleon, First Consul of France, closed all French ports to protect its nascent cotton industry from superior British cotton imports. Many successful Scottish textile companies declared bankruptcy. A discouraged merchant from Perth complained that the cloth business was being "driven at the point of the bayonet."[29]

Napoleon's blockade may have persuaded John to immigrate to America; and friends and relatives in Philadelphia must have urged him to settle there.

The decision to emigrate was a difficult one for John. His father was sixty or so, losing his hearing though still teaching, and still the major caretaker of his  nineteen-year-old son and John's brother—Alexander, deaf since birth. His father needed John more than ever and yet he was leaving Scotland perhaps never to see his father again. He consoled himself that "at least Kittie [Catherine, 22] is so mindful, and Annie [26] so useful to you." [30] He would be useful too; he would send money to his father regularly from Philadelphia.

# 2

## SLAVE SHIPS AND SCHOONERS

ON A BRIGHT SPRING DAY IN 1807, the Grant family was standing on the Liverpool wharves, waiting for the signal to board their sailing ship to Philadelphia. The incoming tide dashed against the barnacled seawall, spraying foam that sparkled in the early morning light and dampened their clothes, to the children's delight. The waves receded, and Hectorina laughed at all the gulls gathering to pick through debris in the black water. Then heavy metal locks opened to admit a large ship. John could tell it was a West Indiaman: its sails were worn, its hull scarred and its crew sounded hell-bent to get drunk. The gates slowly closed behind the vessel, protecting it in a wet basin from the tidal changes of the River Mersey. Stevedores, shouting and cursing over the din, opened the ship's vast hold and rolled out a seemingly endless stream of barrels. John knew they contained riches won on a two-year voyage to Africa, the West Indies and back: barrels of sugar, cotton, tobacco, molasses, coffee.

John Grant "migrated from Liverpool to the United States . . . [and] arrived at the port of New York on or about the Third Day of July, A.D 1807,"[1] according to his alien report. He and his family were possibly on the Liverpool quay in May, as fifty days was the average length of a voyage across the Atlantic.

John had a lean, wiry build, the result of a diet of potatoes, oatmeal and turnips. His height was about five feet six inches, judging from records of Scottish soldiers then,[2] maybe with coloring like his son's— "auburn hair, blue eyes."[3] He was cleanshaven, perhaps with sideburns, his hair, short and natural, like Napoleon's. According to his naturalization document, he never was of "the orders of the nobility," nor had he "any hereditary title."[4]

On the Liverpool quay, John's two-year-old son, Alexander, wobbled on his thin legs, moving cautiously toward a pigeon, stopping to examine a mussel shell. The boy was often sick, with "colds and earaches," but John, at least at that moment, was encouraged, thinking the boy "quite hearty." After a short time of exploring, Alexander held his arms up to be lifted, and John gathered him to his chest. He prayed that Alexander might "be spared to get some years older."[5]

Mary was just five, yet people wondered at "her experience and sense."[6] With her sharp intelligence, she surveyed the scene at the quay: the horse-wagons clattering down the stone wharves, the group of boys in the alley gathered around an overturned hogshead of molasses, the draymen's carts careening around a crowd of brawling sailors, a barrel rolling down some steps with no one in pursuit.

Hectorina, four months old, had wisps of hair just coming in that were not yet the red color it would become. She was not a delicate baby, not jelly in her mother's arms: she was a twisting, squirming baby.[7]

Perhaps John, noticing his wife's discomfort, her shawl fallen off one shoulder, came over to fix it, pulling her close until she smiled. John, having lived in London before, was not overwhelmed by the clamor and tumult of the Liverpool harbor. But he saw that his wife was. She had never travelled beyond Inverness, with its small, east-facing harbor and fleet of seven ships that sailed not the Atlantic, but the Baltic. And rising above that northern port were dry, brown hillsides dotted with green farms, not the smoke-stained buildings of Liverpool.

As the Grants walked the quays, a foul odor assaulted them.

They walked toward the source out of curiosity, holding handker-chiefs soaked in vinegar and camphor to their noses. They found it on George's dock, not far from their own: a ship reeking of vomit, diarrhea and sweat. The vessel had a much larger hold than the usual sailing ship, and a row of small holes along the lower deck that would bring in air. Iron handcuffs, neck chains and collars hung over its side. Mary and Alexander, noticing a continuous stream of casks, puncheons, kegs and barrels rolling into the deep hold, had many questions.[8] Papa discouraged them from any talk about what he knew was a slave ship.

And then, most surprisingly, goats, cattle and sheep filed onto the ship.[9] Mary was convinced she was watching a second Noah's ark. John knew, but didn't say, that the livestock were provisions for a one-to two-year round trip to West Africa and the Caribbean. John had heard that 120 slave ships originated in Liverpool every year, so it was not unusual to find at least one slave ship in port on a given day.[10]

Near the slave ship, men strode about in clunking boots and tall black hats, watching their ships and warehouses suspiciously. John knew they were looking for anyone who might steal cloth, highly valued by Africans chiefs, without which the ship captains would be hard pressed to barter with the slave owners. He could hear them grumbling about the new law that would ban the slave trade as of July of that very year, and he knew they would go to any lengths to continue their trade in slaves. He had heard schemes to fly another nation's flag on their ships or to take their slaving operations else-where. John predicted the Royal Navy would be too busy with Napoleon's fleet to bother with these crafty slave smugglers and that the slave trade would continue unabated.

John left no letters describing his feelings at this leave-taking—neither of the excitement of the life he imagined in Philadelphia, nor of the sadness that tugged at him when he thought of his elderly, "dear, respected parents," whom he would never see again. "Let me hear from

# FRASER / GRANT / MACKENZIE OF FAIRBURN

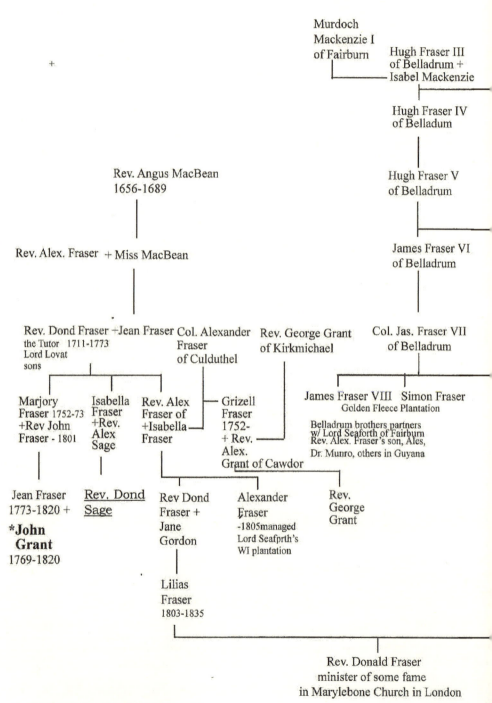

*Symbiotic relationship of ministers with
slave plantation owners and managers.*

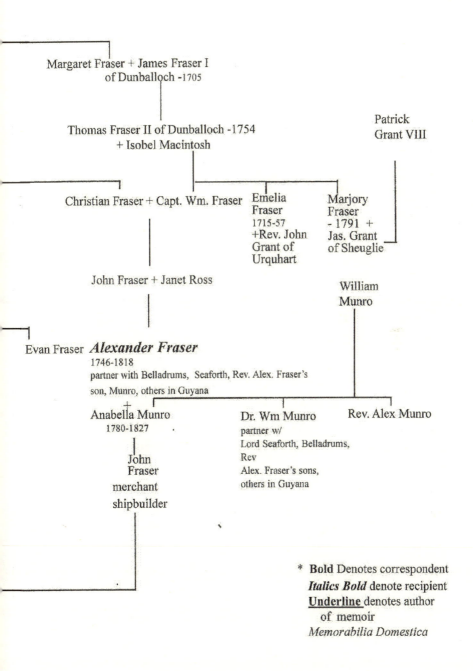

Margaret Fraser + James Fraser I
of Dunballoch -1705

Thomas Fraser II of Dunballoch -1754
+ Isobel Macintosh

Patrick
Grant VIII

Christian Fraser + Capt. Wm. Fraser    Emelia
Fraser
1715-57
+Rev. John
Grant of
Urquhart

Marjory
Fraser
- 1791 +
Jas. Grant
of Sheuglie

John Fraser + Janet Ross

William
Munro

Evan Fraser  *Alexander Fraser*
1746-1818
partner with Belladrums,  Seaforth, Rev. Alex. Fraser's
son, Munro, others in Guyana

Anabella Munro
1780-1827

Dr. Wm Munro
partner w/
Lord Seaforth, Belladrums,
Rev
Alex. Fraser's sons,
others in Guyana

Rev. Alex Munro

John
Fraser
merchant
shipbuilder

\* **Bold** Denotes correspondent
  ***Italics Bold*** denote recipient
  <u>Underline</u> denotes author
    of memoir
    *Memorabilia Domestica*

you once more, my dear Father," he wrote in later years, "let me hear from you once more, my dear and indulgent Mother, let me know how my dear sisters are—Bar [bara] and her husband, Annie and her husband, Kittie [Catherine] and Alexander . . . Do write me—or if you cannot write let one of my sisters write—and you both sign it."[11]

No letters survive from Mrs. Grant about leaving Scotland, either. Indeed, her identity was a mystery. John invariably referred to her as Mrs. Grant in his letters. "Mrs. Grant and all our children continue to enjoy health and in one voice unite in an affectionate regard and love to Father, Mother, Sister and Brother."[12] Or "Mrs. Grant was safely delivered of a son."[13]

A serendipitous discovery of a memoir by a minister, Donald Sage,[14] whose father married an Isabella Fraser, mentioned as one of the two witnesses, "John Grant, merchant." The year was 1784. John would have been just 15 years old. A little girl about the same age, his future wife may have been present too since it was her aunt who was being married. Donald Sage goes on to discuss the heritage of his mother and most importantly, her relations living at the time. One of these was Marjorie Fraser. She and her husband, the Reverend John Fraser of Kiltarlity had three daughters and a son. The daughters emigrated to America. He didn't know where the son was. When I looked through parish testaments, I found a Rev. John Fraser of Kiltarlity, who had died in 1799 without a will. [15] I found "Jean," his daughter had been appointed the executrix and that she had named a "John Grant" as her cautioner (guarantor). Then in a search of parish marriage records I found a "Jean Fraser" who married a "John Grant" on September 14, 1801 in Inverness. [16] John was thirty-two at the time, judging from his birth date in his naturalization papers, but Jean's birthdate remains unknown. John and his future wife were already travelling in the same social circles when he was fifteen years old.

Jean was descended from some scholarly, devout and iron-willed ministers. Among them was her second great grandfather, Rev. Angus

MacBean of Inverness, a major figure of the Scottish Reformation, as uncompromising and stern as John Knox or John Calvin. Refusing to preach Popish doctrine, he was imprisoned and died at thirty-three from the barbaric treatment, shortly after his release was granted by King William of Orange, a Protestant, in 1689.

Her maternal grandfather, Reverend Donald Fraser, was introduced to the chief of the Fraser clan, Simon Fraser Lord Lovat while a student at King's College, Aberdeen. Simon Fraser was a charming but occasionally violent man whose memory would haunt Donald and his descendants long after the chief's untimely death. Recognizing Donald's "capacity and acquirements," Lord Lovat asked him to tutor his sons, a most intimate position within the family, so intimate, in fact, that when Lord Lovat supported the Jacobite cause against the English in 1746, Donald, the tutor, was distraught as he witnessed Lord Lovat's ruin. The chief lost his title, his castle and the clan lands—not to mention his head. The plight of the fatherless boys, to whom Donald "had such strong ties of natural affection, bore heavily on his mind."[17] The eldest of the two would become the acclaimed British general of the North American wars, Simon Fraser. And John and Jean had named their first son, Simon, after Lord Lovat. This is the son, their second child, who died as an infant.

Jean Grant's mother, Marjory Fraser, was the daughter of Donald, the tutor.[18] Marjory's eldest brother, Simon, also named after Lord Lovat, became a merchant in India—where he died as a young man, likely as a cloth merchant in the British East Company—but she and her siblings followed in the footsteps of their forebears, either marrying ministers or, in the case of her brother, Rev. Alexander Fraser of Kirkhill, becoming one.

Jean's father, Rev. John Fraser, was erudite, too. He wrote the engaging and informative description of his parish of Kiltarlity for *The Statistical Accounts of Scotland 1791–99*.[19] A remarkable chronicle of the country at the close of the eighteenth century, the book was the conceptual creation of Sir John Sinclair, who used the term "statistics" for the first time. It covered every imaginable topic: natural features, history, agriculture, manufactures, religion, health, people. When *The Statistical Accounts* were updated in 1835, they ran to twenty-two volumes.

Upon Jean's father's unexpected death in 1800, she and John Grant worked together to settle her father's estate. Her mother was deceased; her two sisters had immigrated to the United States and her brother, to parts unknown.. The lengthy inventory enumerated in Rev. Fraser's Testament lists monies owed him for the remainder of the year from the six heritors in his parish. Though Simon Fraser, Lord Lovat, had lost the clan lands in 1746, the new administrators of his estate were still bound to pay the minister's support. Among the five other individuals listed was Colonel James Fraser of Belladrum, owner with his sons of extensive slave plantations in the West Indies. Since the heritors possessed the sole authority to choose the minister of their parish, the fact that they selected Rev. Fraser suggests they knew he would not confront them about slavery.

It is puzzling that John, the son of a poor master in a charity school, with the annual salary of £10 to £12 Sterling,[20] could travel in the same social circles as Jean, the daughter of a minister—the most respected profession in the Highlands and, in his case, with an annual income of £2,200 Sterling, a rent-free parsonage, a plot of land, and 48 bolls 1 firlot and 1 peck of barley. (A firlot was a dry measure of grain equal to one bushel and one peck is equal to two dry gallons.)

John and Jean may have been distant cousins with a common ancestor generations before. Marriages between Frasers and Grants were frequent. Indeed, though not directly descended from Simon Fraser 11th Lord Lovat (1666–1747), Jean was, at least according to Sage's memoir, the granddaughter of the *tutor* of Lovat's sons. John, however, may have been descended from Simon Fraser 11th Lord Lovat's *wife*, Margaret Grant. Margaret ( –1729) was the daughter of Sir James Grant 7th of Freuchie (1616–63). Freuchie was another name for the Grant Castle, which according to my family's legend, had been connected with John Grant.

In John's time, however, the link between his and Jean's families was Alexander Fraser, Jean's cousin. Alexander was a well-to-do merchant in Inverness involved in thread manufacturing, among many other interests and a partner of the Frasers of Belladrum and Lord Seaforth of Fairburn in the management of their West Indian slave plantation. Alexander Fraser and his more famous son, John Fraser Esq., Provost of Inverness, were witnesses at Mary Fraser Grant's baptism.[21] John's letters to his parents from America were always addressed to Alexander Fraser, too, making it clear that his father and Fraser had remained good friends since their early teaching days in the SSPCK charity schools. Fraser may also have been an investor in John's merchant enterprise, supplementing Jean's family money.[22]

John and Jean were of the evangelical branch of the kirk, strict followers of John Calvin, as opposed to the moderates, consisting of devotees of the Deist Scottish Enlightenment. The couple was present at a meeting in 1800 in Tain where the evangelical Northern Missionary Society was founded. John was named to the board of directors and Jean's uncle, Rev. Alexander Fraser of Kirkhill, was elected president.[23] The goal of the Society was "to check and gradually annihilate the inhuman traffic [of slaves] and to ameliorate the condition of their unhappy people."[24] In the meantime, however, the group sanctioned slavery as a necessary evil.[25] Indeed, shortly after the meeting in Tain, Alexander, the younger son of the new Northern Society president was to head off to Berbice to manage Lord Seaforth's cotton plantation.[26]

The moderate branch of the kirk, made up of slavery sympathizers, based their support of slavery on the bible verse Isaiah 46:24. Slavery was defined as "lawful captivity." They reasoned that just as taking captives in a *righteous* war was legal, so slaves *righteously* bought were legal. John Calvin, the ultimate authority for the kirk, defined *righteous*: "He is said to be the *righteous* possessor who is the lawful possessor."[27]

Crossing the Atlantic was a risky undertaking anytime—even in spring and summer. Men often wrote their wills before boarding a sailing ship, though John, whether characteristically optimistic or unrealistic, did not. The captain could be incompetent, the crew drunk or mutinous, the vessel unseaworthy; its masts and timbers could be broken by gales, its sails torn—or it could be captured by a hostile nation.

Swarms of war ships patrolled the Atlantic and Caribbean after slaves revolted in 1791 in the lucrative French Caribbean colony of St. Domingue (now Haiti). Sparked by the French Revolution two years earlier, seven-hundred thousand slaves rose up and murdered their white masters. Civil war continued between factions within the free people of color, blacks and whites, even after the French revolutionary government abolished slavery in all French colonies in 1793.

Nothing could have frightened the colonial powers in the Caribbean more than a successful slave revolt against greatly outnumbered white plantation owners, whose only weapon was brutal punishment for the infractions. Britain, France, Spain and Holland increased their naval presence in the Caribbean, making sea travel more dangerous.

Such travel became exponentially more dangerous when Napoleon, by then the French first consul, hankered after a French empire in America, following his acquisition of the Louisiana Territory from Spain in 1800. The linchpin of his strategy was to reassert control over St. Domingue and restore a slave economy. Napoleon sent soldiers and seamen to the island in 1802, who were successful—until the rainy season began. Yellow fever broke out in all its virulence, as it had every year since the small ship *Hankey* made a stop in St. Domingue in 1792 for fresh water. The *Hankey* had carried the bedraggled remnant of some three hundred well-meaning but delusional British abolitionists who had intended to set up a free colony of blacks and whites in Bolama, Guinea. When most sickened and died mysteriously in Guinea, a handful of remaining people boarded the *Hankey* to go home, not knowing that their water casks carried the eggs of the mosquitoes infected with yellow fever. Wherever they stopped to refill their casks as they island-hopped from the west coast of Africa to St. Domingue to Philadelphia, they distributed the eggs, causing in 1793 the most deadly outbreak of yellow fever that Philadelphia was ever to experience.[28] In following decades, yellow fever would take thousands of lives annually in the hot rainy season in the West Indies, Philadelphia, and cities on the Atlantic coast.

The emancipated blacks in St. Domingue had developed immunity to the disease in their homeland in West Africa. They had only to sit back and watch the mosquitoes do their work for them. As the French soldiers died in ever-larger numbers, Napoleon sent ever more soldiers. Privately, though, he told his finance minister, Barbé-Marbois, "I already consider this colony entirely lost." When only seven thousand of a total of sixty-five thousand troops remained, Napoleon ordered his decimated army back home. Jean-Jacques Dessalines, the elected governor, declared the island the independent republic of Haiti two years later, whereupon he incited a massacre of whites. A handful of Bolama Society survivors accomplished what no European country had yet—the defeat of the most powerful army in the world.

And by doing so, they helped enlarge the United States of America. "Louisiana had been destined to supply [St. Domingue]," Barbé-Marbois recalled. With the loss of the island, there was no need for Louisiana; indeed, it would sap the French of resources to keep it. Dejected and in need of cash, Napoleon gave up on an

American empire altogether, selling the Louisiana Territory to the United States in 1803. "I need a lot of money," he told his negotiators as war between France and Britain erupted again after a short peace. "Louisiana will give me the initial funds for war on the English scoundrels." He would rather have Louisiana in the possession of the weak American nation—only a string of settlements clinging to the Atlantic coast—than in the possession of his enemy, the British, already possessors of a large North American empire.[29]

Napoleon's spiteful decision of 1803 did France no good and Britain no harm. And it provided the United States with a platform from which to extend its reach westward across the continent. American merchants, among them the Grant and Ridgway families, would take advantage of the convenience of cheap water transport to market their commodities, from the Ohio River to the Mississippi to New Orleans and back. The mosquito carrying malaria would also travel this route. (While yellow fever and malaria are both mosquito-borne diseases brought from Africa, malaria is caused by a parasite carried by *Anopheles gamblea*, which was not discovered until 1897 by a Scottish doctor in India; yellow fever is a viral disease carried by *Aedes agypti*.)

Ironically, the successful slave revolt in Haiti resulted not in the emancipation of more slaves in other islands or nations, but in the enslavement of still more people. Native Americans were shackled and removed whenever they blocked American westward expansion. And slave planters in the American Appalachians, mostly Scotch-Irish, as well as wealthier Tidewater planters, would enlarge their cotton plantations—staffed by enslaved laborers—west to the Mississippi. Slavery would exist in southern Illinois until the 1863 emancipation—despite Illinois' admission to the Union as a free state.

The European continent would belong to Napoleon until 1815, but the British ruled the seas after 1805, when the Royal Navy destroyed a large part of the French fleet at Trafalgar.

John may have been waiting for just such a victory before setting out on an Atlantic crossing for the risk of hostile attacks on their schooner would be lessened and thus, their family safer.

The Grants were finally given permission to board their ship. In a familiar protocol, the captain gave John the manifest to check against his own list, making sure the numbers of barrels and crates of calicoes and muslins, Irish linens and ginghams, cambrics and cassimeres, that were marked JG matched his own count. In their ship cabin, their home for the next seven to eight weeks, the family likely found their trunks in place and tried to adapt to the cramped quarters.

They may have been the only passengers, as was Philadelphia merchant George Cooper,[30] a small importer of British manufactured goods, who sailed from Liverpool to Philadelphia in 1800. Because British ship owners made more money carrying freight than people, they took on few passengers. According to the manifest of Cooper's ship, the *Wm. John*, the freight of wealthy Philadelphia merchant, Charles Wharton, left little room for Cooper, his trunk and a few crates of merchandise.

The Grants watched crew members climb up the masts, unknot the sails and bend them to the yard arms. The lock gates of the wet dock slowly opened, the sails filled and the vessel moved down the River Mersey to the open sea. However, no sooner was the journey begun than the ship inexplicably slowed to a stop near other merchant vessels, perhaps as many as one hundred fifty, stretching over several square miles of ocean. Parliament, in 1803, required merchant vessels to sail in convoys escorted by the Royal Navy, in order to prevent French seizures.[31]

Sometime later, a ninety-eight-gun, two-decker war ship, its cannons protruding from ports on both decks, arrived. And then a squadron of smaller, fifty-gun men-of-war ships joined the anchored merchant schooners and their sailors. The two-decker vessel hoisted a signal flag and fired its cannons in several ear-splitting crashes, followed by a thunderous salute of guns from the smaller ships. The Royal Navy escorts rounded up the merchant ships, and the group began to move as one body—or at least that was the hope. Convoys often became dispersed, "not seeming to pay the least attention to the Commodore's signals," one captain complained.[32] Nonetheless, convoys proved to be effective against attack.

As the Grants sailed off, they must have tried to keep their thoughts on the glowing reports of America brought back by Scottish soldiers from the North American wars. The Grants believed they were obeying God's plan in migrating. As Grant wrote in a letter, "He is bringing about his own designs of love and mercy, tho' we cannot comprehend them."[33]

Philadelphia was known then as the Athens of America. While by then the city was no longer the capital of the United States, the new capital, Washington, was no competition: it was without any port for trade and was a marshy, unappealing town, only partially built. Philadelphia was still a busy port, maintaining brisk trade with Britain and Europe, which was remarkable for a young nation so recently a dependent colony.

The ship's upper deck had begun leaking water into the Grants' cabin after a heavy downpour, demoralizing the usually cheerful family. Afterward, nothing would dry out. Everyone was out of sorts, parents scolding, children complaining, Hectorina screaming.

When they went up on deck, the leaden skies and water greeted them in all directions, without sight of a landmark or lighthouse, and the wind whipped them until they nearly froze. There was never any relief from seasickness, and terror kept them in its constant grip as the ship pitched and rolled. Cockroaches got into their clothes'[34] and there were the never-ending diapers to be washed.

On a clear night on deck, perhaps it seemed to them that the light of creation shone through countless pinholes in the black dome of the sky. At such moments, the Grants' trials seemed trivial to them.

As the voyage neared its end, John must have been looking forward to seeing his old friend Hector Kennedy. They had been children together in Urray and had dreamed of immigrating to America together. Hector had been in the United States for fourteen years, nine of them in Philadelphia, sharing a warehouse with another Scot, a Quaker, at 73 South Front Street. John planned to use it, too. Business had been very good. Wouldn't Hector be surprised to see his namesake, Hectorina Kennedy Grant, now six months old, sitting up by herself and laughing at everything?

After more than five weeks, the Grant children announced they'd seen land barely rising above the horizon and green-tinged. Soon they were south of the Capes of Delaware, taking on a pilot for the last 110 miles to Philadelphia. Because the tide was going out, the ship had to anchor off a sandy island and wait for the tide to change.

While the Grants waited in the still air they were shocked by the bright light and searing heat of the June sun, unpleasant weather for Scots accustomed to a northern climate with an almost constant cloud cover.

The tide at last in their favor, the pilot took the helm, and the ship began its slow ascent up the Delaware, steering away from the shallow western shore of New Jersey and around the shoals that were not on the charts. This took an interminable two weeks of seeming to hardly move at all.[35] As the Grants became captivated by the rich wildlife and numerous marshy inlets emptying into the Delaware estuary, its water so calm, the family noticed their seasickness was gone. When the Delaware Bay narrowed to a twisting river, a crowd of Philadelphia-bound ships sailed in tiers next to them, some close enough to touch.[36]

It was from a ship abreast of theirs that the captain and the Grants may have learned of a June 22nd military engagement off the coast of Norfolk, Virginia. Speaking through a horn, the captain of the adjacent ship conveyed the bad news:

BRITISH WAR SHIP FIRED AT
AMERICAN FRIGATE SEIZED AMERICAN
SEAMEN MANY AMERICANS KILLED WOUNDED[37]

John would have to wait for details until after he arrived. For now he was too happy to worry over whether this limited engagement would lead to more violence. When the Delaware River took a turn to the west, John glimpsed Philadelphia at last. William Penn's green squares that John had heard tales about were obscured by the many warehouses. Yet rising above the jumble of wooden structures and wharves jutting out into the water was the steeple of Christ Church, signifying to John that God was present, even in this land more than three thousand miles from home.

# 3

## The Athens of America

As the Grants' ship drew close to the Philadelphia wharves on July 3rd, 1807, the tangle of masts, yard arms and spars assumed distinct shapes: brigantines, frigates, schooners, sloops, barks, ketches, three-masted-Indiamen—a staggering variety. No steamships, yet, to shroud the harbor in smoke.

From yard carriages, derricks and capstans, the mariners' songs tumbled across the water, their songs throbbing to the beat of the yo-o heave ho. Tipplers at the Crooked Billet, Penny Pot and Blue Anchor Taverns joined in with jolly refrains.

The Grants were in high spirits as they pulled into the harbor. Compared to the colossal Liverpool wet docks and high granite sea walls, where they'd started their journey, the two-mile-long Philadelphia waterfront was human in scale, and quirky in an appealing way. Buildings were stacked not quite squarely on top of the ones below; one dock listed; and the wharves were so jam-packed with outbuildings, sheds and warehouses that to find a path around them would seem an impossibility. Incongruously, there was a tall brick mansion right at the water's edge, with a white balustrade on its roof.[1]

This helter-skelter appearance of the waterfront, though,

belied the city's bustling commerce and the wealth of its elite merchants. The seaport was the third busiest in the world, behind only London and Liverpool.[2] On any given day in 1807, there might be a hundred or more vessels, many in the West Indian trade at the docks, moored in the river or ready to launch.[3] Merchant and ship-owner Stephen Girard left an estate of $7.64 million ($192 million in 2014 dollars) when he died in 1831;[4] Jacob Ridgway (more about him later), $3.5 million;[5] and a few others, such as Thomas Cope, were millionaires.[6] Yet this image of opulence was also deceiving; there were very few merchants with such fortunes. Profits came from taking huge risks, with the flip side of huge losses. Without a safety net, many a merchant sank into insolvency. Though there was a middling sort, made up of artisans and shopkeepers, they, too, were few, and their position was just as unstable. Most people were very poor: they included mariners, unskilled laborers, occupants of the almshouse and the unfree, such as slaves, apprentices and indentured servants.

This contrast of poverty with abundance was most obvious on the waterfront. Stephen Girard's and Jacob Ridgway's mansions stood next to taverns and boarding houses that served seamen and prostitutes in crowded alleys. "Hell-town" lay a short distance to the north, and the shipbuilding district around Dock Creek, close by in the south. In these two low areas, yellow fever took the most lives in bad summers, sometimes five out of eight in one building.

The Grants debarked at the southern end of the wharves, near Dock Creek, onto Water Street. It was a puddled and rutted dirt track, and the air above it was foul-smelling, close and stifling. Finding stairs in a narrow alley, they trudged up several flights, their legs wobbly after eight weeks of sea travel, and emerged onto light-filled, cobbled Front Street. They understood, after their climb, why it had seemed from the water as if the buildings rested on the shoulders of those below: Front Street ran along a steep bank, parallel to the river and fifty feet above it. William Penn had meant for the bank to remain open (except for his mansion and a few others), leaving the view of the river mostly open. But he was a shrewd businessman and finally bowed to practicality, allowing buildings to straddle the bank, provided granite steps were constructed at mid-block intervals for public access from Front Street to the river.[7] Wharves were then built out into the river on fill made of stones and soil to support still more buildings and a new road, Water Street—which at first was simply known as the road under the bank.

Although there were many taverns that served overnight guests, Mansion House would have been more appropriate for a family of young children. Their fellow Scot, John Melish, cartographer and former merchant, had stayed there in 1806.[8] Perhaps they learned that he had stayed there from Scottish acquaintances. In any case, this is where they were bound.

Because they had several large trunks, the Grants took a carriage to the hotel. Once loaded, their carriage clattered along Third Street to Spruce Street and turned into a semi-circular drive. They were taken aback by the size and elegance of the building. It was the largest in Philadelphia, occupying an entire block, with a frontage of one hundred feet and an interior of sixteen thousand square feet.

Only three years before, in 1804, this palatial brick building, surrounded by ornamental gardens, had been the home of Senator William Bingham. When the Binghams had both died, insolvent from the Revolution, their mansion was leased to William Renshaw, an hotelier from England. All the fine French furnishings, the statues and mirrors that graced the public rooms when the Binghams had lived there had been sold at public auction. Nonetheless, the room proportions and walls, in the style of Scot architect Robert Adam, remained as beautiful as ever. There were four large rooms in the three-story part of the house, a one-story wing on each side and a flight of elegant marble steps, seemingly unsupported.

The Grants were such a small family at the time, with just three children, the oldest being five, that they would have wanted only one room. A trundle bed and a cot would have been all they needed for the children, because baby Hectorina was accustomed to sleeping with John and Jean in the large bedstead. Since it was summer, the canopy of the four-poster bed would have been dressed with a short lace cover and a muslin skirt. At dinner, the terrapins were in season, as Renshaw announced in the *Gazette*: "A fine Sea Turtle will be dressed and served up on the publick table at the Mansion House Hotel, on Tuesday next at 3 o'clock. Tickets to be had at the bar until Monday evening."

The next morning the Grants awoke to a distant din of brass bands, drumming, loud speeches and the shots of cannons. In their exhaustion of the night before, they had perhaps forgotten that the next day was July 4th, the anniversary of American independence. They rose quickly and navigated the few blocks to the State House, where the music seemed to originate. Packed into the crowd, John lifted Alexander to his shoulder just in time for him to see the Second City Troop go by on horseback, in full regalia—bright blue uniforms, gold braid, high hats—while Jean tried to restrain the girls from chasing and patting a dog. Snatches of languages foreign to the Grants hummed around them. American flags flew from the tops of the many pitched tents; African-American fiddlers, leaning back in their chairs under the tents' shade, played favorite songs, some of them Scottish in origin—"Barbara Allen," "Auld Lang Syne"—and of course "Yankee Doodle." Quaker songs did not exist; for them music was the devil's creation.

Tired from excitement, the family might have strolled back to Mansion House, taking detours at will, amazed that, in this unfamiliar town, they never felt lost, thanks to the elegant grid plan and the wide streets. They may have admired the ample shade of trees, the cleanliness of the streets and sidewalks, the abundant water, the little streams running down all the gutters. There was, however, the ubiquitous odor of privies, one behind each building. In Scotland, though, the odor had been much worse, and privies were not removed until the 1860s in Inverness.

The modesty of the uniform, attached brick houses, accented only by the marble of the lintels, sills and scrubbed steps, might have appealed to the Grants' sense of decorum. The many passers-by on the sidewalks greeted them affably, surprising the Grants, who weren't used to such friendliness from strangers. Others, dressed in grays and browns, the women in dark bonnets, the men in wide brimmed black hats, might have given them sober but nonetheless cordial nods; the Grants no doubt guessed they were Quakers.

Back at Mansion House after the July 4th parades, they surely must have eaten. Servants would have served a light supper in their room. They were not very hungry because they likely stopped at one of the many vendors on the street corners, selling a wide variety of food. Pepperpot soup, a West Indian specialty, was a Philadelphia favorite. The calls of the black women selling it echoed down the streets. Even ices were available, a French introduction. Many French had immigrated to Philadelphia from St. Domingue after the slave revolt in 1791, bringing their taste for fine food.

Perhaps later in the afternoon, the Grants found their way to the hotel's brick-walled garden. In its heyday as the Binghams' mansion, the gardens had fragrant lemon, orange and other citrus trees, moved from a greenhouse to the outside in the summer, and gravel paths winding under shade trees in an English-park-like setting. Although many plants would have been unfamiliar to the Grants, maybe there were a few spruce and firs to remind them of the Scottish gardens that the West Indian cotton planters had installed on their estates when they came home.

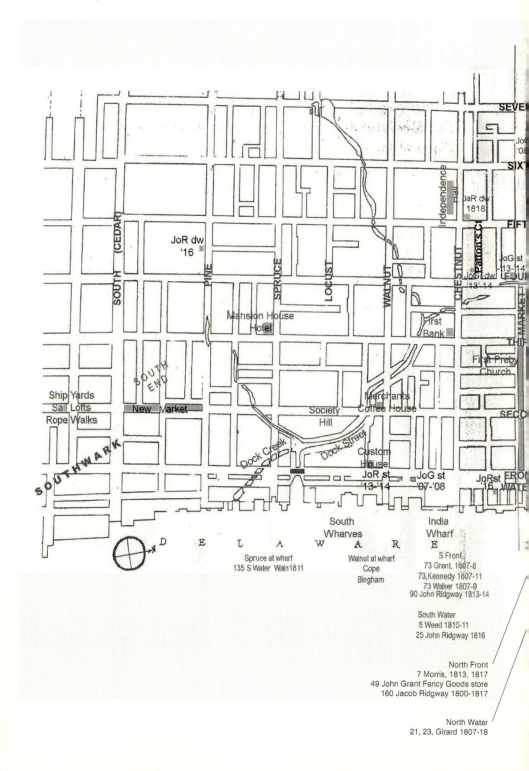

*Philadelphhia in John Gramt's Time 1807-1818*

In the evening the skies were ablaze with fireworks, some very close to Mansion House. Viewing the pyrotechnics, John and Jean were struck with awe at the privilege of being in this civilized city, participating in this novel republican experiment. By the last burst of sparklers, the children had nodded off, and John and Jean had to carry their sleep-limp bodies to bed.

John had been waiting all day to show Jean the article he'd read that morning in the Norfolk Herald about the British firing on the American frigate on June 22nd. He handed her the newspaper, and she read quickly, skimming: "The whole of this country is ripe for revenge . . . It is fully ascertained that this is not at all an affair of accident."[9] Perhaps Jean proffered a dose of common sense: "They're just words, John. Don't borrow trouble." They lay down together, John putting his arm around her, pulling her close to him. A sense of well-being must have infused his body, slowing the rhythm of his breathing, and he fell asleep.

That night, Thomas Cope, Quaker shipping merchant and West Indian trader, wrote in his diary of his relief that there had not been protests on July 4th like the one that had occurred in Northern Liberties right after the two frigates affair. He'd feared they might have turned violent. "The Fourth passed without any act of violence or outrage," he wrote. "Fears were entertained that when the fumes of liquor were added to the effervescence already induced by the recent transactions, mischief would be the consequence."[10]

The next day, John decided to find the warehouse and store of his childhood friend from Scotland, Hector Kennedy. It was just a few blocks from Mansion House at 73 South Front Street,[11] but he decided to walk the entire two-mile waterfront to get a sense of the curved harbor lying between the two industrial areas of Southwark and Northern Liberties, from Cedar Street (now called South Street) to Vine Street.

Walking along South Front Street, he caught glimpses of Water Street and the wharves down the alleys that had been dictated by Penn. The first two blocks of the wharves, from Cedar to Spruce, were crowded with sail lofts, ship chandleries and makers of rope, masts and anchors, with boarding houses for mariners, small stores and dwellings tucked in between. In the next few blocks, East Indiamen, the largest class of ships, were tied up at the wharves, their masts towering over the buildings. At an opening at Spruce Street, he caught a glimpse of Walns' wharf and their two- and three-masted West Indiamen abreast of the docks. From Walnut to Chestnut, Thomas Cope had his counting house and brigantines and frigates. Smaller retail and wholesale shops and taverns lay between Chestnut and Market. No tall ships were visible. From Market to the Arch Street landing, where ferries to New Jersey left regularly, he saw the five-story brick mansion with the white balustrade they had seen on their arrival. He knew now that it belonged to Stephen Girard. Next to it he caught a glimpse of the tavern called the Crooked Billet. Here, too, was Girard's fleet of tall ships. Front Street continued on a bridge over Arch Street, the only street that was graded to the river, with no steps necessary. Jacob Ridgway's tall ships poked above the buildings between Arch and Race. Race to Callowhill was occupied by small buildings and was known as Hell Town. Here, yellow fever claimed the most victims each summer and fall in its boarding houses, breweries, taverns, flour storehouses, pump and block makers and chandleries. Tall ships were visible again near Callowhill at West's boatyard—the ships being either built on dry docks or repaired.

Suddenly the crash of a cannon thundered across the water. John was afraid that the British had fired on another American frigate. Crowds collected on the wharves, many with spy glasses. Some men summoned sloops and sailed out to investigate, or climbed to the rooftop balconies of their wharf mansions. Then, to John's great relief, an East Indiaman, likely packed with Indian and Chinese cottons, rounded the river bend. The cannon shot had been its greeting after more than a year's absence from home.[12]

John retraced his steps, walking south to the intersection of Front and High Streets (High is now Market), where he'd earlier seen the sign that read Walker & Kennedy, denoting Hector's store and that of his partner from Glasgow, the elder Emanuel Walker, son of the toll collector at Port Glasgow.[13] It was what was called a bank building: a warehouse on the basement level, which faced Water Street and the river, and the upper story of the same structure, which opened onto Front Street. They loaded and unloaded cargoes on wharves, Ross being the most common, which suggests that they didn't own a wharf.[14] Compared to the shipping merchants near them on what were called the India wharves, they were small traders. After so many years in West Indian trade, John had hoped to see them become more prosperous, and he worried about his own prospects.

Hector and John greeted each other with some trepidation: after ten years apart, each wondered if the other had changed. John always mentioned Hector in his letters home: "Mr. Kennedy and Mrs. Manwaring [his sister] are well."

Hector had been thirty-three and John twenty-eight when they had last seen one another, and neither had been married then. Hector had been engaged in West Indian trade with Emanuel Walker since his arrival in the United States in 1797.[15] After the awkwardness of this first meeting, the two men fell into old familiar patterns, their questions and answers spilling out so fast, they talked over one another. Hector asked about many topics: his family still in Scotland, the cloth industry in Glasgow, tobacco lords (whether they were still so wealthy since cotton exports from the American south had surpassed tobacco by then), their friends in the West Indies—James Grant, Donald J. Mackenzie, Donald McIntosh, R. Chisholm and Kenneth McRea.[16] John asked practical questions: how to find a house and store to rent, and where to advertise his cloth. Hector invited the Grants to his home on 17 South Spruce Street[17] to meet his wife of less than a year, Hannah Summers, [18] and John invited Hector to Mansion House to meet his wife and children, especially Hector's namesake.

As John surveyed Hector's and Emanuel's warehouse, he could see that Hector had been working hard to make room for John's cloth. But the space was going to be tight. There were large crates of Jamaica rum and Madeira wine, hogsheads of Virginia tobacco, over a hundred bales of raw Tennessee cotton and trunks of German ticklenburg, a coarse linen used for mattress, bolster and pillow covers, slave clothing and bags this last addressed to Emanuel. Over the years of their partnership, they had also imported Demerara rum, Queens ware, coffee, sugar, ship timber, rice and the medicinal herb ginseng, prized in China.[19] Except for the ticklenburgs their business had a different focus than the fancy-goods store Grant planned to create. There is no evidence that a partnership was offered or that Grant would have wanted one. But John gladly accepted their offer to use their warehouse until December 1807.

After the men discussed the latest reactions of traders to the affair of the two frigates, Hector suggested he and John might go to the City Tavern, where they could converse with other merchants and peruse out-of-town newspapers in the subscription room. The City Tavern, established in 1773 by an elite group of shipping merchants, had fallen out of favor after the capital of the United States moved from Philadelphia to Washington in 1800. But for a quarter of a century, it had been a glittering venue for discourse, balls and celebratory dinners for those who belonged. Members were wealthy Philadelphians who could afford the annual subscription fees of £25. Hector, a relatively small-time merchant, would not have been among this exclusive group. He could only use the public coffee room downstairs.

If the tavern had lost some of its cachet as the best hostelry in the country, it had been reborn as the home of the first stock exchange in America. The Board of Brokers, as they were known, met upstairs in a private club atmosphere, where they conducted the business of buying and selling commercial paper, creating the credit, capital and liquidity so necessary to the conduct of international trade. They made Philadelphia the financial capital of the United States. In the tobacco-filled upstairs room, they bought and sold federal debt— still considerable after the Revolutionary War—as well as bills of exchange and shares of stock in new companies such as the Farmers and Mechanic Exchange Bank and the Insurance Company of North America and in such infrastructure projects as canals, bridges and turnpikes to the west, which the Grants and the Ridgways, would later use.

An elaborate system of wires and hanging bells allowed the merchants, without interrupting their activities, to call for a messenger to bring them lists of current commodity prices, stock prices in Amsterdam or ships in harbor. They would then exchange views over a jug of ale or, more often, coffee. Coffee from Spanish colonies had always been more popular in Philadelphia than tea from the East.[20]

Hector and John walked to the brick tavern at Second and Walnut, just a block from Hector's Front Street store and warehouse. Earthy aromas mingled with the sharp scents of exotic spices escaping from the tavern's cellar kitchen, unidentifiable to John but enticing. As they climbed the white marble steps, protected from the elements by a broad awning, the buzz of conversation inside escalated into angry shouts and table-pounding. John guessed tempers were raised over the affair of the two frigates and the advisability of a federally imposed embargo. After entering through the Federal-style doorway with its carved pediment and fan light, all John could hear was the clanging of pewter plates and tankards and the footsteps of servers rushing up and down the stairs to and from the kitchen.

They were met by the host and directed down the central hall to the door of the public coffee room. Ship captains, small merchants, insurance salesmen, politicians, artisans and farmers regularly gathered there to buy and sell cargoes, form new partnerships or make arrangements with ship captains—and, of course, to enjoy good food, drink and conversation. Standing at the door of the coffee room, John scanned the space. It was obvious that no decorating expense had been spared. Fine upholstery and rich wood carving announced to him, as only the coffee houses in London had, the gentility and stylish taste of the members.

Almost immediately, Hector caught the eye of some merchant acquaintances, who gave him a signal to join their table. After hearty greetings and introductions, they studied the menu for dinner, the main meal of the day. It was a dizzying list of entrees and confections, mostly unfamiliar to John. Hector had been in Philadelphia early enough to have tasted the cuisine for which the French *emigres* from St. Domingue had set the standard. He urged John to try turtle soup, a Philadelphia specialty, made from fast-disappearing, three-hundred-pound green sea turtles from the West Indies, along with *Shad a la Touraine*.[21] And because it was a hot summer day, he said that John must try the French pineapple-laced punch and the crushed-ice cup.

When the conversation veered from the laissez-faire theories of the Scot Adam Smith, in which John was thoroughly versed, to American politics, he was at a loss to follow the thread. He understood there were two political parties, President Jefferson's Democratic-Republicans and their opponents, the Federalists. But certain groups had crossed lines in recent years, blurring the parties' identities. Each explanation that Hector and his friends offered threw John into deeper confusion. Finally, since he knew the Federalists were against the embargo, John said that he must be a Federalist. The men joked that one could tell a man's politics by his menu choices—Jeffersonian Democratic-Republicans ordered French dishes, and Federalists, English ones, [22] and that therefore John must be a Democratic-Republican, because he had just consumed French dishes and was staying at the Mansion House Hotel, where French menus were just as *de rigueur* as they had been when the Binghams lived there.[23] John quipped that his having just drunk two pints of English porter confirmed he was a Federalist. The convivial banter continued until someone proposed a resolution, which was seconded and unanimously approved: whatever the politics of the food, Philadelphia was surely the gastronomical capital of the world.

Meanwhile, at a table in one of the Board of Brokers' private rooms upstairs, on the floor above Hector and John, Thomas Cope was making a list of provisions he had to load on his brig to the West Indies. For his meal that afternoon, he had ordered boiled meat and vegetables, simple English Quaker fare, and was waiting for it to be brought upstairs. Fortunately, a new chef had been hired at the City Tavern in 1785, Edward Moyston, "who offered cuisine 'in both the French and English taste.'"[24] Cope's idea of a fine meal was fresh boiled beef, mutton steaks, turnips, potatoes, beets and cucumber pickles.

Cope was considering the prospects for shipping merchants in general and for himself. The ability to trade freely with Europe was in much graver danger than Hector and John could have guessed. Cope had just breakfasted a few days before, on July 2nd, with one of Jefferson's intimate friends, and had learned that war could be imminent. "We are on the verge of that greatest of all evils," he confided to his diary. "Should my expectations be baffled & the total loss of all I possess ensue, I shall not be more severely chastened tha[n] I merit. Such is the unbiased opinion I entertain of my own unworthiness." [25]

Downstairs, as the diners began to leave, petitions were circulated, with import merchants signing one opposing an embargo, and owners of new factories of cotton cloth from Northern Liberties signing another favoring an embargo; protection from the competition of British manufactured cloth would greatly benefit the fledgling industries there.

The issue dividing Britain and the United States was the British practice of impressment—forcibly kidnapping unsuspecting civilian men off the street or from foreign ships into the British Navy, notorious for such vile conditions that no man would do it willingly, except for the officers. A Royal Navy war ship needed some five hundred seamen, as gunners and sailors. Punishments meted out by captains for perceived disobedience were severe—even life threatening. The pay was abysmally low, the food inedible, and shipboard conditions were appalling, with each seaman allowed just a fourteen-inch space for his hammock. The ill-treated men deserted at the first opportunity, some few joining the American Navy. To fill the warship's constant need for seamen, as the bitter battles against Napoleon's fleet raged on without end, British Navy captains forcibly boarded American ships, alleged that many of their seamen were deserters from the Royal Navy, and seized them—even tearing up men's American citizenship papers, claiming they were false. Such impressment had triggered the June 22nd two-frigate incident between the British and American Frigates.[26]

Assuming all would turn out well for him, John proceeded with his business plan. He placed advertisements in a newspaper called *Poulson's American Daily Advertiser* by the end of the month, listing his place of business as 73 South Front Street, Hector's store.

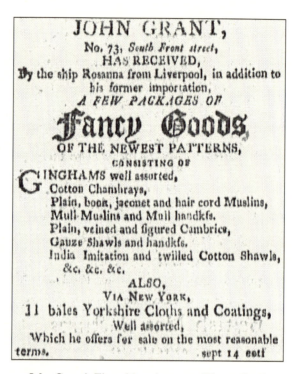

*John Grant's First Advertisement of Fancy Goods*

With the limited space available to him, he did his best to display his fancy goods appealingly. Nothing could have prepared him for the troubles that lay ahead.

# 4

A New House on Mulberry Street

IN THE END, PRESIDENT JEFFERSON decided against war and in favor of a more measured response to the two-frigate affair. The American Navy, even with the help of privateers, could never compete with the English fleet of warships, the largest in the world. In December 1807 he sent an embargo bill to Congress, which was passed before the end of the year. U.S. customs agents detained any merchant ship trying to export cargoes, such as Cope's and Jacob Ridgway's, or imports, such as John Grant's. Commerce stopped altogether as a result of an American self-imposed embargo.

As Douglas Irwin wrote in a 2005 article in the *Review of International Economics*, "The United States was by the middle to late 1808 about as close to being fully shut off from international commerce as it has ever been during peacetime." This "major shock to trade" caused growing conflict between the two political parties—Federalists, who were out of power, and Jefferson's Democrat-Republican party. It caused the near secession of New England from the Union. Wheat, cotton, flour, tobacco and rice lay rotting in the fields. The wholesale prices of imports rose by thirty-one percent in Philadelphia during the embargo, causing economic suffering for many in America and famine for John's family in Scotland and those in the rest of Britain and Europe.[1]

And yet the embargo did not stop the lawless behavior of the belligerents, Britain and France, who had been fighting a world war off and on since 1792. France's ploys to draw Americans into a three-way war continued, as did Britain's impressment. There was very little defiance of the embargo by exporters. Some ship owners applied for and received letters of marque, which granted them permission to arm their vessels as privateers for the U.S. Navy. And a few exporters smuggled goods from secret ports in Vermont, Maine and Canada toward the end of 1808.

Jacob Ridgway, uncle of a figure to become central later in this story, moved with his family to London to supervise his firm's interests while his partner, Mr. Smith, watched the business in Philadelphia. When Jacob was appointed United States Consul at the Port of Antwerp, Holland, he was able to save "many extensive and valuable consignments of American goods" belonging to the Smith-Ridgway firm from capture and "vast sums [were] realized." For example, learning of the seizure of one of the firm's vessels, Jacob hurried to Paris to secure "papers of release" from Napoleon and arrived back in Antwerp in time to stop the captors from taking the shipment.[2]

John Grant, living on credit, could not go to Europe as Jacob Ridgway did to protect his shipments, nor could he afford to speculate in cotton goods before they were sold out in American cities. The effect of this interdiction of trade on his business was disastrous. In 1809, he wrote Alexander Fraser, his Inverness mentor, his father's friend, and Jean's cousin, about the previous year of the embargo. "Everyone who had money . . . launched into speculation in foreign goods—This City bought out in India Goods and pretty much so in Newyork Boston & Baltimore." [3]

Thomas Cope was one such speculator. On a trip to Baltimore in July 1808, he "purchased near 400 packages of Calcutta and German piece goods . . . Merchandize is daily advancing in price &

large fortunes making by speculations," Cope wrote in his diary. He recounted one such example of frenzied speculation in a November 1808 entry. "T. & S. sold 4 bales muslins at $2.55 per ps to J. & T.—bot them back again at $3; sold to J. & L. at $3.25 who sold them to the same J. & T. at $3.60 who again sold them to T. & S. at an advance & the latter have lately sold them at $4.25. This is a small scale—many have embarked not only to the am't of thousands, hundreds of thousands."[4]

The embargo lasted for fifteen months, from December 1807 to March 1809. When it was lifted, prices fell precipitously causing great economic distress. This period was especially difficult for John because he had to move out of Hector's warehouse and find a store for himself. He located an empty shop at 49 North Front Street[5] amid other shops selling notions and fancy-goods (fine muslins and gauzes), just two blocks from the shopping center at Second and Walnut Streets. He saw Stephen Girard often, because Girard had a greengrocer at 43 North Front Street. Girard had put his wife, whom he claimed still to love, in the Pennsylvania Hospital for the Insane, while—as rumor had it—he carried on an affair with his housemaid. Girard had one sightless eye and was grotesque-looking; his hair was pulled into a pigtail at the back of his neck, in the style of the old sailor that he was. His French accent was still pronounced.[6]

The embargo was not the only obstacle John faced in his first year in business for himself. Before he arrived, a new kind of dry-goods dealer had appeared and seemed to be flourishing: the auctioneer, whose business was organized as a partnership or a corporation.

Bypassing the regular channels of small British importers like John, auctioneers bought large packages of textiles, finished clothing, even "fancy goods," brandies, wine and hardware—almost anything that had accumulated in factories and wasn't spoken for. For cash on delivery, the British charged the auctioneers lower prices than they did commission agents like John, who bought on credit and paid twelve months later. The auctioneers announced sales of their dry goods days in advance in the newspapers and sold them in large lots, sometimes including partially damaged ones, to the highest bidder.[7]

Though the auctioneers worried him, John reminded himself that he was selling to the retail customer, not the wholesale trader. He could give his clients personal attention, suggest they feel the hand of the fabric and inspect each piece for flaws. And he could take the time to arrange his goods in new combinations to appeal to the customers' craving for novelty and discovery. One day his mahogany table might be set with highly polished glass and silver on one of his shimmering damask cloths, and on another day with dainty lace and ribbons, silk hosiery, fine handkerchiefs and kid gloves, suggesting a lady's preparations for an evening of dancing or cards at an elite salon. He could tell them that he had personally visited the British mills that had produced the fabrics.[8]

While the auctioneers advertised lots that might contain some unknown amount of "fancy goods," John's ads listed each kind of cotton fabric individually: "Just received by the *David Green* from Liverpool . . . the most fashionable patterns in great variety . . . for sale on the most liberal terms," he wrote in one advertisement. "Mull muslins" with a very fine weave; "cambric muslins," closely woven, for linings, shirts and dresses; "leno muslins," soft-textured, for underwear and domestic uses; "chambrays," a plain weave cotton with colored warp and white filling; "ginghams" from Scotland—the finest in the world—in checks or plaids for curtains and women's and children's clothing; "cambrics" of cotton or linen with varying thread counts, both "plain and figured," some daintily "veined," with one or more warp threads omitted; "Gauze Shawls . . . India Imitation & twilled Cotton Shawls" and "Ladies [riding] habits."[9]

Gentlemen in cutaways and ladies in empire-waist dresses, silk bonnets and delicate shoes went browsing and shopping for hours along Front Street, though there were fewer of them since the U.S. capital had moved to Washington. These were no doubt among John Grant's treasured customers.

In March 1809, the Embargo Act was withdrawn and a less draconian Non-Intercourse Act passed. All the British cloth that had been accumulating in the mills during the embargo immediately flooded American markets, driving prices down. "I shall lose better than £1,000 Sterling$^g$" John wrote Alexander Fraser, his mentor as a boy in Inverness and a likely investor in John's business. The value of his goods was reduced so much "that by the Stock I had on hand (being purchased when goods were high last fall) I shall lose more than the profit made on the others . . . India goods are now selling 25 prct . . . lower than last fall . . . I shall (if God spares me) recover myself . . . but it will be but moderate until a free trade with the continent be restored to us Americans." (Underlining is John Grant's. His swift adoption of an American identity had taken no effort at all because independence from England had always been close to a Scotsman's heart.) John added in a postscript: "I cannot write my Father at this time. JG"[10] It may be that he was unable to write to his father because he didn't wish to share this bad news.

John didn't mention to Alexander Fraser that, in the midst of these business difficulties, he had bought a house at 266 Mulberry Street (now Arch Street).[11] Two rooms deep and three stories high, the brick house in the block west of Ninth Street stood on a twenty-by one-hundred-foot lot with a separate, two-story frame kitchen (with the upper story being the living quarters of the servants), and unspecified outbuildings behind. One would have been a privy or necessary while others may have been milk, wash and smoke houses. He bought another 120-foot-deep lot and building west of Tenth Street for stabling his horse and cow and for housing a cart, the distance not being a terrible inconvenience to John and his family. His optimistic view was that, though the house was at the northwest edge of the fashionable district now, the pace of building west was so brisk, it would soon be near the center.

The square footage of a house has been used by some historians to place a person in a social class. John's house, at eighteen by thirty-two feet, yielded about two thousand square feet, not counting the two-story kitchen behind, placing him in a class of "middling merchants." Since wealth had become more concentrated in the hands of fewer people since the Revolution, there was a wide difference in living standards between a middling merchant, such as Grant, and a wealthy one, who might have had a house forty-eight by forty-eight feet, totaling 6,912 square feet, not including a two-story back kitchen, stables, a coach house and other outbuildings.[12] John's income during the embargo might not have been much more than that of a master tailor, who in 1800 earned £134 a year, and a master tailor might also own his house and have an indentured servant.[13]

Occupants of houses on the Grants' block of Mulberry Street included single women and gentlemen, a sea captain and some merchants. However, next door at Number 268 was a tanner and currier business, from which the smells of decomposing animals escaped. And across the street was a soap boiler, who took the fat the tanners scraped from the animals' skins and rendered it into soap. The air for the Grants must have been foul-smelling at times, but little different from the air surrounding expensive homes in Society Hill, where the same kinds of businesses existed along old Dock Creek.[14]

Furnishing all the rooms in their large house would have been prohibitively expensive for the Grants, and no doubt some rooms remained bare and others, sparsely furnished. The drawing room of a family was conventionally almost empty with only sofas and chairs. Tables were kept in another room and only retrieved when the need arose.

On occasion, Scottish friends might have gathered at the Grants' home on Mulberry Street for an evening of music and dancing. John would welcome the guests as Jean beckoned them to the white damask-covered dining table, where she poured Chinese tea sweetened with Barbadian sugar into china cups from her British silver tea service. Carefully she passed a cup and plate to each guest, along with a silver spoon and linen napkin, as servants moved about with trays of custards, whipped syllabub and tarts. Twelve Windsor chairs were pushed to the edges of the two downstairs rooms for older friends to rest, while the Ingrain carpet had been removed for dancing reels.[15] Cider, sherry, Madeira, port wine, champagne and claret were arrayed on the sideboard. The flames of the candles and fires were reflected in the polished silver and looking glass and alighted on a dancer's flushed cheek and a fiddler's rosined bow. Smoke from tobacco encircled the guests in a pleasant haze of laughter, with bursts of spirited singing—"wawking the faulds, I wish you would marry me now . . ."

On the afternoon of Monday, June 3, 1811,[16] Jean and the children were in the back sitting room of the new house. Long shadows from the sunlit plants on the windowsills spilled across the floor. The servants were chattering and clanking pans in the kitchen behind, preparing supper. Soon John would come home for supper, bringing hickory logs for the kitchen. "I presume that I have wrote you that our fuel is wood, chiefly oak and hickory," he wrote his parents. "To keep three fires in the most Economical place for six months will cost near £30, Ster$^g$."[17] To his children he said it was wasteful to burn wood, because he remembered how scarce it was in Scotland and how much work it had been for him to dig the peat for his family's fuel. His children laughed because he always said the same thing when he brought wood home, and because to them, wood was not scarce at all.

There was no need for fires in the house's main rooms in June. Rather, cooling ploys were needed. "You can form no idea of the extreme . . . heat in Summer," John wrote his parents, "An European Climate is a heaven on earth." They threw open the windows, took down the curtains, covered the lolling chair with white linen and rolled up and stored the Ingrain rug, which they might have bought nearby, in Northern Liberties, from the first American carpet manufacturer.[18]

Hectorina, age four played on the bare wood floor with a cloth doll Jean had made, undressing her, laying her in the cradle John had built, then singing a lullaby, that was followed, in the very next moment, by waking and dressing her—with the routine being repeated many times. Two-year old Rachel Magdelaine, supposed to be taking a nap, was kicking and singing nonsense songs in the crib Jean kept downstairs. Jean was pregnant again. Sometime in the fall, she wasn't sure just when, they would go to the First Presbyterian Church on High Street to have Rev. Wilson baptize the new baby, as he had all the children, the oldest three for a second time. There were several Presbyterian churches in Philadelphia then, but the Grants chose the most mainstream one and the one their friend John McKenzie and family attended. Looking like a Roman or Greek temple, it stood opposite the meat stalls on High Street.[19]

In the front parlor, nine-year old Mary had begun practicing the piano that June afternoon—which might have been built by John Behrent, the first American piano maker, at his factory in Northern Liberties.[20] She was dutifully going through the scales and pieces her music teacher had assigned when she allowed herself a little recess to play the Scottish tunes her teacher forbid. Jean may have dropped her sewing and stared out the window, as she remembered the fancy step-dancing she and John had performed to perfection at the Northern Meeting parties in Inverness. Alexander, six, was studying his Latin lessons, perhaps in the front parlor because the family's library of 33 volumes[21]—alas, unnamed—was kept there. When he finished Latin in a few months, he would start Greek, in preparation for what his parents hoped would be a career in the ministry.[22]

Mary pulled a small, baize-covered desk and chair from the wall to the center of the back sitting room to write her letter to her aunt Catherine; all the furniture—twelve chairs, many tea tables and a large dining table—lined the walls of the room.[23] Mary remembered that her aunt, John's younger sister, was a spinning teacher for the SSPCK,[24] and she may have remembered helping aunt Catherine wind a skein of flax with her when Mary was youmg. Spinning seemed old-fashioned to Mary now; the family chose cloth they liked and a tailor made their clothes.

Jean brought Mary a quill, a small bottle of ink, a blotter and several sheets of paper so she could practice her penmanship first. Mary had studied "epistolary correspondence," grammar, spelling, and definitions at Stephen Addington's School on High Street, according to a newspaper article about the instruction offered there. Other subjects were composition, prose and poetry. And though it was a school for young ladies, she had also studied "Orthography, Arithmetic, Geography and the use of the globes."[25]

*Philadelphia 3 June 1811*

*My dear Aunt,*

*It is with the greatest pleasure I sit down to address you a few lines I never wrote you before I now take the liberty of addressing you per-haps you might expect a more complete letter from me but I hope your affection will excuse any faults you may see in it.*

*I attend one of the first schools in Philadelphia which is kept by a Mr. Addington an Englishman where I learn Reading, Writing Arithmetic Geography and Grammar of which class I am in the 1ˢᵗ of all except Arithmetic.*

There has been some gentlemen from England Missionaries in this place on their way to the East Indies. There has been one Mr. May among them who is much concerned about children visiting most of the schools in Philadelphia exhorting the children about Religion he has got a whole trunk full of books which the children in this place hath given to him to take to the children of the East Indies.

For my part of the ministers I have heard I like Dr. Haughton and Mr. May the best the former of which is a settled Baptist in this place the latter of which I have been speaking about.

Mrs. Manwaring [Hector Kennedy's sister] is very well and Mr. Kennedy the same.

I wish'd you would come over & see us we would be very glad to see you. I entirely forgot to tell you that I was learning Music I can play a few Scotch songs but my teacher will not allow me play any tunes but keeps me wholly upon lessons.

Alexander is coming on very well he can read very well Hectorina is only at her letters & Rachel Magdalene is a fine playful child. Alexander is very subject to the ear-ache and a severe fever in consequence of it but Hectorina is as fat as butter and Rachel Magdalene is a beautiful child her face is as fair as a lily her cheeks are as red as a rose. Hectorina & Rachel are both red hair'd This is the first time I ever wrote a letter except one I wrote to Mamma when she was at New-York the next will be to Rachel Robertson.

Mr. John Mackinzie's at Augusta and we have heard from him lately at which time he was well. Papa and Mamma is very well Papa and Mamma give love to you all. I hope my grandpapa and grand-mamma and my relations and friends are all well we are all well give my love to grandpapa and grandmamma and Aunt Anne. I can say no more at present.

 I remain My Dear Aunt
   Your affectionate niece
   Mary F Grant[26]

It's nice to get a view inside the Grant's family life through this letter. We hear the charming voice of a precocious child of nine and we also see the remarkably close Grant family connectedness even across an ocean. Though Mary would never see her aunt again, she continued to write her aunt until two years before her death.

John indentured two servants,[27] at The Old London Coffee House, the former slave market at Front and High Street which continued as a venue for obtaining servants, even after slave trade was abolished in 1807. They would be "bound" to work for him until the debt of their fares were paid and he would feed, house and clothe them until then.

After a light supper that evening, supper, Jean took the children upstairs. There was just one bedstead because they were expensive. Even when the Grants were a family of eleven, they owned only four. Sisters and brothers shared beds in most Scottish families, except the wealthy. John and Jean would take the youngest child to bed with them, while cots on wheels, or hurleys, were rolled out from under the bedstead for the older children.[28]

A month or so after Mary wrote Aunt Catherine, John sat down to write his first known letter to his parents, full of praise for his new country but containing very little personal news, and without the tobacco they expected, both of which must have been disappointments to his parents.

*12 July 1811*

*My dear parents,*
*Had you known (you say) as much of this country 20 years ago as you now do you would come here yourself. Undoubtedly this is a great Country, and will be a most powerful Country. Nature intended it should be so—In extent it is immense—and from the variety of*

*Climate it affords not only the necessaries but the luxuries of life in great abundance. The Eastern States Commonly called New England produces Indian corn, wheat, rye, barley oats & potatoes. But commerce & Fishing is their chief support. The middle States to which this State Pennsy a & New York belong, exceed all the rest for commerce & Agriculture. The Southern States vary, Maryland & Virginia are famous for Indian Corn & Wheat but the Staple article of Virginia is Tobacco. The State of Kentucky is famous for Corn—Cotton and Tobacco grows also—North Carolina the same but the Staple article is Timber, Pitch, Tar & In South Carolina & Georgia India Corn grows but Cotton & Rice is their grand commodities; State of Louisiana (New Orleans the Capitol) is first for Cotton (& famous for Sugar, good for Tobacco & Sweet Oranges). The Climate of the Middle & Eastern States are the best In the Southern States it is very severe.*

*This Country has been very prosperous since the revolution till within these four years past. The restrictions on honest industry by the wickedness of European governments and the debility of our own—our trade is destroyed and I am sorry to say not likely to mend for some time. With real pleasure should I send you a little Tobacco but the risk is— that none can arrive with it. Were it[found with] them on their arrival in a British Port [ it would render] all their baggage seizable.*

*Remember me to Mr. & Mrs. [Alexander] Fraser at Inverness when you see them. In my next I shall let you know what prospect I have of going home.*[29]

He didn't write that he knew he had no prospect of returning to Scotland. Only Alexander Fraser knew that. In his 1809 letter to his old mentor, he'd asked him to persuade John Smith [his lawyer] to procure . . . a discharge from the Court of Session tho' I have little to fear from the word of it, yet it would be a great satisfaction for me to have it."[30]

The issue John referred to was his conviction by the Scottish Court of Session for his non-payment of £548.14 to James Hamilton

Sr. & Co., a Glasgow broker. The court had decreed that John be arrested at first sight upon returning to Scotland. As a further affront, the court permitted Hamilton & Co. to take the £548.14 commission owed John by Finlay Duff & Co. of Glasgow.[31] He couldn't bear to tell his parents he would never return to Scotland.

# 5

## A FORTUITOUS MEETING

RELATIONS CONTINUED TO DETERIORATE between the United States and Britain and France, as Britain and France persisted in harassing American ships and violating the young nation's neutrality. More than fifteen thousand sailors were impressed by the Royal Navy to sail their ships. Commerce with Europe was nearly paralyzed. "The sanguinary war in Europe . . . has now raged for upwards of 20 years," Thomas Cope wrote on February 18, 1812, in consternation and amazement.[1]

John wrote his parents in a state of alarm six days later, on February 24, 1812. "Business is at a stand . . . The only hope we have left is from a change of Ministry in England which is expected as soon as the Regent gets into Power. Before Congress met, we were in expectation they would as soon as they met take off the restrictions [on trade] in common with the [British]. And come to some arrangement with GBritain, in place of that we had some high war resolutions entered into—Probably you would be alarmed, but you need not fear—it will take some time before we are ready—probably six or seven years—If our great big threats would frighten you, we should like it better than go to war. . .It is with much concern I have, there is a scarcity of grain in GBritain . . . Cruel times prevent my having [the] satisfaction of being useful to you . . . Yours till death . . . John."[2] Food riots had swept Europe as grain lay rotting in fields in America.

Four months later, on June 1st, President Madison called for a declaration of war on Britain, which the House of Representatives immediately approved. On hearing the news, Cope was apoplectic: "Congress has hazarded the bold measure of war against England. I can scarce credit my senses . . . The country is without navy or army. The Govt. has destroyed the Bank of U.S [in 1811]. . . At the same time that the Secy. of the treasury has issued proposals for borrowing 11 millions to meet the demand of the current year & yet they threaten a war of aggression with a nation which possesses upwards of one thousand ships of war, ready at a brush to sweep the last remnant of our commerce from the ocean!"[3]

Tragically, three weeks *after* Madison's declaration of war, a letter from the British Government arrived in Washington offering to lift all trade restrictions and cease impressment. Having resolutely declared war, Madison could not turn back without a loss of face. Indeed, Americans attacked British warships before Britain had even heard of its declaration. For the next two years, battles were fought not only at sea but on American soil, along the Canadian border, in the Northwest Territories (all land west of Pennsylvania, east of the Mississippi and northwest of the Ohio River) where Native Americans took the side of the British, and even in the nation's capital, where the British set fire to the White House.

After two and a half years of war, neither country had accomplished anything, except that the U.S. had proved it was a country to be reckoned with on the world stage, and French-born Stephen Girard was hailed as an American patriot: he had bought the defunct First Bank of the United States and single-handedly financed the war.

In December 1814, the warring nations signed a peace treaty in Belgium, but the news arrived in Washington too late—again—to prevent a January 1815 sea battle in the Gulf of Mexico. Though it was a boost to U.S. morale to have routed the Royal Navy there, this victory changed nothing.

After the end of "the great shaking," when all "the foundations of the earth [were] out of course,"[4] as one contemporary described the more than two-decade-long French Revolutionary and Napoleonic War—indeed world war—commerce was expected to recover. Yet the outlook was bleaker than ever. Many banks had been chartered by state legislatures to fill the vacuum left by the former Bank of the United States. Chief among the causes, the state banks loaned money on excessively liberal terms to settlers buying western land, fueling a boom. When the state-chartered banks went to exchange their bank notes for gold or silver at the new Second Bank of the United States (created in 1816), however, they were refused. Banks and ordinary citizens began to hoard metallic specie, state banks foreclosed on land they'd financed in the west; settlers slid into bankruptcy, as banks stopped lending. The state bank notes were worthless. Eventually, gold and silver disappeared from circulation

Thomas Cope wrote in his diary about his experience with the state-chartered bank of Pennsylvania. "With more than ten thousand Dollars which I have idle in the Bank of Penna. I have this morning been driven to the necessity of borrowing a few Dollars in silver from a person in my service to go to market."[5]

Even the wealthy China, East and West India merchant Robert Waln, uncle by marriage of a person to enter the story later, was in critical financial straits. In July of 1819, with cheap British cloth flooding the American market after the war, Gideon Wells, manager of Waln's cotton factory in Trenton, informed Waln that he was prepared to shut down the mill if the ticken's, or ticklenburgs, an Eagle Factory matress-covering specialty, which were then selling at a "dreadful [high] price,were no longer accepted by merchants."[6]

Because there are no extant letters of John Grant between 1812 and 1818, one has to infer from his family's frequent changes of address that their situation was becoming increasingly desperate. Perhaps he didn't want to worry his father with the news; he would have been incapable of lying to him. On December 28, 1812, six months into the war, a newspaper advertisement gave notice that the Grants' Mulberry Street house was for sale,[7] and the 1812 Philadelphia Directory (address listings of city inhabitants) showed his and his family's dwelling as 2 Patton's Court, a crowded warren off Fourth between High and Chestnut Streets.[8]

After the end of the war, cheap British cloth flooded the market, underpricing John's goods bought before the war, just as was the case when the embargo had been lifted in 1809. He moved his store twice, first to South Fourth and then to North Third,[9] less expensive to rent but also less visible to consumers than 49 N. Front Street. And the family moved from their Patton Court shambles once more in 1816, and then again in 1817, first to a house at 211 Callowhill Street between Fifth and Sixth Streets, and next to another on the same block (number 173—all are pre-1858 numbers). This was the barely respectable north end, next to foul-smelling tanneries, textile dye works, brothels and taverns. Callowhill Street near the river had been hit hard by yellow-fever epidemics in 1793 and 1805, but the Grant family's homes were too far from the water for the infected mosquitoes to fly.

By 1818, it was clear that Philadelphia's days as the busiest American harbor were over. It was too impractical for sailing ships to take two weeks to "tide it up" the Delaware Bay, within sight of land the whole time, yet not be at their destination. New York's harbor was more convenient. And, unlike the Delaware River, it didn't freeze. By the early 1820's, New York's exports and imports were valued at more than twice those of Philadelphia.[10] Many Philadelphia merchants moved to New York, including Hector Kennedy, who married a widow there in 1817.[11] His first wife, Hannah Summers, had died in 1809,[12] and his partnership with Emanuel Walker had been dissolved in 1811.[13] Hector's subsequent employment history was checkered with insolvency and legal problems. He died in 1828 at his home in Trinidad de Cuba[14] at the age of sixty-four, a good life-span for the time.

While living on Callowhill Street, John met a neighbor, Caleb Ridgway, fifteen years younger, whose lumberyard was on the next block west, on the same street. Caleb's misfortunes were as severe as John's but different in kind: he was an industrialist who had been helped by the embargo, not an importer. But his woolen factory was burned to the ground for a loss of $20,000 in 1815, with the cause thought to be arson.[15] Then his lumberyard on Callowhill at John Street suffered losses as shipbuilding in Philadelphia declined.

It was in the vicinity of John's house and Caleb's lumberyard that John learned that Caleb was wealthy Jacob Ridgway's nephew. The name, Jacob Ridgway, would have been well known to any merchant in Philadelphia. He was an inspiration to Caleb—for better or worse—because of his successful career as a land speculator. Jacob Ridgway was no paragon of virtue, and neither was Caleb. In 1804, Caleb had been disciplined by the Quaker Upper Freehold Meeting in New Jersey, at first for his "neglect of attending our Religious Meetings," and later because he was "charged with taking strong drink to excess, using profane language, deviating from plainness in Dress and Address." Finally, after he showed no lasting remorse, "the meeting unites in proceeding to disown him."[16]

Wealthy as Jacob Ridgway had become from trade, he made the majority of his fortune from speculating in real estate in western Pennsylvania and in Philadelphia, where he built cheaply constructed houses for immediate income.

Thomas Cope was not an admirer of Jacob Ridgway. He told a story in his diary of "some personal altercation about property" between Jacob Ridgway and Stephen Girard. "'I could buy and sell you,'" bragged Uncle Ridgway, to which Girard coolly replied, "'I could buy you, Mr. Ridgway, but I don't think I could sell you.'"[17]

Caleb and his uncle were descended from an English Quaker, Richard Ridgway, who had arrived with his family in America in 1679, a few years before William Penn. He was Caleb's third and Uncle Ridgway's second great-grandfather.

Richard, the immigrant, born 1648–50, was the younger son of a noble English family from Wallingford, Bucks in England. He settled first on the west side of the Delaware River at the head of Bile's Island, near Penn's manor, and then moved to Burlington, New Jersey.[18]

Richard's son, Thomas, born in England in 1677, moved to Little Egg Harbor, New Jersey, a commodious and protected port on the Atlantic Ocean. The Ridgway family, at least this branch of a very large family, remained there for many years. Thomas was "an Elder of the Friends Meeting at Little Egg Harbor, and was much esteemed in the community."[19] A similar testimony about his son, John, born in 1705, described him as: "a benevolent spirit, his heart and his house were open to entertain his friends and others . . . assisting the poor . . . In conversation with men of various ranks he demeaned himself with a becoming gravity which rendered him truly worthy of esteem."[20]

Thomas and his son John were owners of slaves and had a lucrative business carrying grains, food and lumber in their own ships to British sugar plantation owners in the West Indies. John Ridgway found "it necessary to follow the sea for a time," according to the testimony, "yet by attending to the divine principle of grace, he was preserved from that extravagance in his conduct and conversation too prevalent in men in that business."[21]

Nevertheless, "many individuals of the various generations of the Ridgway family," wrote the historian of Little Egg Harbor, Leah Blackman, "have been the possessors of an abundance of the riches of this world, and to so great an extent has this been the case that the name of Ridgway seems to carry with it a tingle of the 'Almighty dollar.'"[22]

# RIDGWAY

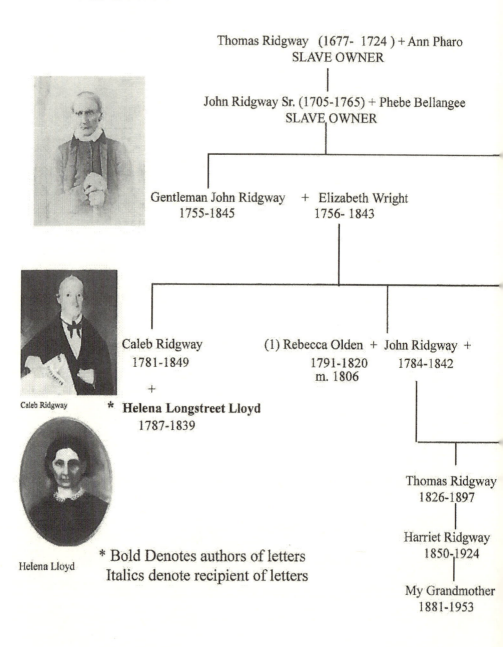

Thomas Ridgway   (1677-  1724 ) + Ann Pharo
SLAVE OWNER

John Ridgway Sr. (1705-1765) + Phebe Bellangee
SLAVE OWNER

Gentleman John Ridgway   +   Elizabeth Wright
1755-1845                            1756- 1843

Caleb Ridgway          (1) Rebecca Olden  +  John Ridgway  +
1781-1849                    1791-1820              1784-1842
                                    m. 1806
        +
*  **Helena Longstreet Lloyd**
1787-1839

Caleb Ridgway

Thomas Ridgway
1826-1897

Harriet Ridgway
1850-1924

Helena Lloyd

\* Bold Denotes authors of letters
Italics denote recipient of letters

My Grandmother
1881-1953

"Uncle Jacob Ridgway"   + Rebecca Rawle
1768-1843

Jacob Ridgway

* **Mary Fraser Grant**   * **David Ridgway**   *Sarah Ridgway*
1802-1839          1791-1841          1779-1872
m. Jan 1821

+                  +

Sarah Wilmans      Nicholas Waln
m. 1823           1763-1848

During the American Revolution, the British attacked the Little Egg Harbor home of John Ridgway's rebel son, known as Gentleman John, born in 1755. His nickname helped to distinguish him from many others of the same name in Little Egg Harbor.[23] The British, having learned that Gentleman John had hidden rebels in his house, burned his home, orchard and crops to the ground. Gentleman John barely escaped with his life after a sword fight at his doorway.[24] His experience was so distressing that he gave up trade with the West Indies and moved inland to the rural town of Crosswicks, New Jersey. Gentleman John was the father of Caleb and the older brother of Uncle Ridgway.

Gentleman John's oldest child, Sarah, born in 1779, married Nicholas Waln, who lived just across Crosswicks Creek.[25] Sarah projected so much empathy and kindness that many people opened their hearts to her in letters, especially Caleb's wife, who had known little affection from her own family. Of Sarah's six brothers, only one of them, David, ever wrote her letters from Illinois. All but the youngest, Thomas, speculated in cheap land in Illinois when the government opened up the state for sale in 1818. By early 1818, two brothers, John and David Ridgway, had settled there.

After Caleb and John Grant confessed their precarious financial situations to one another, Caleb told Grant about his "Brother John," as the family called him. Brother John, born in 1784, had moved with his wife and family of five children to an Illinois farm near the town of Carmi, on the Little Wabash River, in 1818, and was happily settled. And David, a still-younger brother of Caleb's, then unmarried, had been in Illinois longer, speculating in land, trading with New Orleans and getting rich, as he wrote his sister. Caleb and John Grant decided to try their luck in Illinois, as well.

Reluctantly, one imagines, Caleb's and John Grant's wives and children agreed to make the thirteen hundred-mile journey of unknown perils together. The U.S. had bested the British in the

*Gentleman John Ridgway 1755–1845*

Northwest Territories in the War of 1812 and had forced most of the Native Americans living there to cede their land, falsely promising the indigenous tribes that they could have land in Northern Illinois instead. Many Natives distrusted the promise and fought the white settlers for the land, attacking their cabins and killing the family of one man while he was out farming.

The American government's colonization of the West was like the earlier English conquest of Scotland. Indeed, the SSPCK was almost as active in its efforts to convert Native Americans to Presbyterianism as it had been actively seeking to convert Scots in Highland Scotland.[26] The Natives and Highlanders were both thought to be barbarians by the SSPCK, needing Christianity and pacification.

John and Caleb and their families began to make preparations for their journey, including liquidating their businesses. In April 1818, Caleb advertised his lumberyard for sale.[27] Two months later, in June, John Grant announced the closing of his cloth business in *Poulson's Advertiser.*[28] With hopeful hearts, they and their families readied themselves to leave Philadelphia.

# 6

---◆———◆———◆---

# "Perils by Land and Perils by Water"

---◆———◆———◆---

On an April evening in 1818, in the Grants' rented rooms at 173 Callowhill Street, the warming fire had dwindled to embers, and the damp smell of the thawing earth outside was seeping through the windows, making John and Jean shiver. At the washstand, Jean poured frosty water from the flasket into the basin and repeatedly splashed her face until all the dust from the nearby brick factory had been removed and her skin was clean. Then, seated before her dressing table and looking-glass in the light of the quickly disappearing candle, Jean had let down her long hair, sprinkled here and there with white. And perhaps in a habit of many years, which, by its mindless repetition, prepared her for rest, she brushed it over and over until she lost count. The thorough brushing also served to clean it, for drenching her head in icy water to wash it in winter was too forbidding.

Not wanting to waste the embers, John shoveled them into the bed-warmer and ran the long-handled brass pan slowly between the sheets. Eager to enjoy this warmth, they hastened to get snugly settled on their feather bed under layers of quilts before the sheets cooled. Spread about the room were the cradles and cribs for the younger children and trundle and field beds for the older children, all of whom were fast asleep. Jean gently scooped up baby Catherine from her place on their bed and moved her limp slumbering body to one side so she and John could lie together. With the winter bed-curtains drawn at last, Jean rested her head on John's shoulder as he drew her to him. He had been saying for some time that the family's livelihood depended on leaving Philadelphia and moving to the far western frontier. And now, her mind being settled, she told him for the first time that she was willing to go.

Jean had not wanted to leave the East. Alexander was advancing quickly in his Latin and Greek studies,[1] requirements for a degree in divinity at a school like the Presbyterian College of New Jersey in Princeton. There would be no such instruction in Illinois. Jean, perhaps even more than John, had wanted Alexander to follow in the footsteps of her forbears, all men of the cloth. Abandoning his study of the classics was a "serious disappointment" for Alexander, John wrote his parents.

Fearing she might lose her resolve she decided not to tell John she was pregnant; she would wait until they had left Philadelphia. Her mind may have turned to worrying about her unborn baby's safety on such a perilous journey until she remembered a verse in Matthew that she had memorized as a girl to please her father. Perhaps knowing John would like to be reminded of it, too, she recited it aloud. "Do not be anxious about your life . . . Look at the birds of the air, they neither reap nor gather into barns, and yet your heavenly Father feeds them." Taking comfort in God's promise, they lay quietly together until their breathing became regular and and deep and they fell asleep.

❖━━━━❖━━━━❖

Those who had gone west strongly advised others to leave in the spring, or no later than early summer, while the Ohio River was still full from snowmelt, the current strong enough to float a flatboat at a steady rate. One of the most knowledgeable and immensely popular books of such advice was Morris Birkbeck's *Notes on a Journey to America*, published in 1817 and followed in May 1818 by *Letters from Illinois*.[2] Birkbeck's practical suggestions and informed descriptions of his journey were invaluable to Americans on the move. "Twelve thousand waggons passed [us] in the last year"[3] on the turnpikes as land opened up in Ohio, Indiana and Illinois, he wrote. His book went through eleven editions. Birkbeck, an English Quaker with a command of geology and the humanities, had immigrated to America in 1817 from Surrey, intending to found a farming community in Edwards County, Illinois, to be called Albion (just ten miles north of the Grants' and Ridgways' destination of Carmi). Cheap land in America was a powerful lure to Birkbeck, tired of forty-year leases of land with no hope of advancement to ownership. He and his party had travelled by stagecoach from Norfolk, Virginia, to Pittsburgh and from there on horseback through the trackless wilderness and prairies of the western states to the location of his projected town. Nonetheless, he recommended that families travel west from Pittsburgh by boat down the Ohio, rather than by horseback. He listed the necessaries to bring—bedding, tents, agricultural tools, axes for clearing land, seeds, cattle and horses, guns to defend against wild animals, pirates and Indians, and especially cash. There was no specie in the west because of the devaluation of state-chartered bank notes. He warned about the filth of most taverns and the scarcity of labor and listed the expenses they could expect before they could operate at a profit. Believing the autumnal "agues and bilious fevers" were caused by miasmas in the river valleys, he urged settling in the uplands and building log cabins on the prairie rather than under the sunless, wooded copses by streams. In entertaining sketches, he characterized the people he had met, from refined and educated company to drunken sailors and vulgar French trappers, and depicted the wide variation in economic circumstances, from those who travelled in a coach-and-six and a comfortable flatboat with private apartments to the barefooted family walking with their possessions on their backs, leading one cow, and then huddled on a crude raft floating down the Ohio, open to the elements.

John knew of Birkbeck and may have read his books. "A Mr. Burbek," he wrote his parents, is "at the head . . . of upwards of 200 families from England who came over last year and are settled" in Illinois.[4]

Both John and Caleb Ridgway knew that delaying a journey west past mid-summer could mean encountering an impassable, ice-choked river or one so low that becoming stranded on a sandbar or a rock ledge was a distinct possibility. But some unavoidable, unnamed circumstance must have delayed their departure until October: perhaps it was difficulties in concluding their business affairs in Philadelphia; the late delivery of Conestoga wagons, oxen and teamsters hired to haul their merchandise and furniture; or an overdue ship carrying the German redemptioners John had bound to work for him in Illinois.[5]

Finally, with the wagons packed, they were ready to leave. By then there was an autumn chill in the air. John lit a fire of birch logs in the back sitting room and sat down at his candle-lit writing desk to write his parents about his decision, paper and ink before him and goose quill pen in hand. It was the evening of September 27, 1818.

*Very dear and much respected parents,*
*We are on the eve of leaving Philadelphia and going to Illinois*
*Territory about nine hundred miles from this place [an underestima-*
*tion] . . . Illinois is one of the best States in this Country in point of*
*soil and climate and is getting settled very fast—no doubt we shall be*
*deprived of many privileges that we enjoyed in this great City—but*
*providence seems to appoint that the residence of our family should*
*be some where else, and who can say to him what dost thou—he is*

*bringing about his own designs of love and mercy, tho' we cannot com-*
*prehend them . . . May we look to him where efficatious blessing can*
*make every thing work together for good.*
    *Ever Your dutiful and Affectionate Son*
    *John Grant[6]*

A few days later the family began their journey west. John swung his whip toward the horses' hindquarters, and the wagon started with a jolt, perhaps throwing Jean and the children backward. The older ones screamed in delight—Mary, sixteen; Alexander, thirteen; Hectorina, eleven; Rachel, nine; John, seven; Janet, five—though Jane, two, and Catherine, seven months looked at their mother with alarm. Settled on blankets covering the floor of the wagon with their precious piano next to them—the first to be brought to Illinois—the children must have thought this was the start of a great adventure. The darkness of the early morning would have only added to the drama.

Caleb followed in another wagon with his family: his wife Helena and their six children, the youngest, Emma, seven months old, about the same age as the Grants' baby, Catherine. Perhaps the Grant and Ridgway children of similar ages switched wagons to play together.

Caleb and John had very different temperaments. John was devout and conscientious; Caleb, aloof and rebellious. But Caleb could give Grant a great deal of useful information about Carmi, a new town and quickly growing. He assured Grant that "Brother John", his wife and children were very content on their Carmi farm of a few months or so. And it was Caleb who had told Grant how to find German redemptioners to help him with constructing his new store and log cabin home. Brother John had paid for thirteen German redemptioners to work for him for four years, and the arrangement was working out well. Grant had made contact with two or three young Germans eager to have their passage paid to the United States, and he bound them to work four years for him.

The wives, in contrast to the mismatched husbands, were very close. Jean, the elder, and Helena had discovered they had much in common as neighbors on Callowhill Street in 1817 and 1818, especially as their children were about the same age and had begun to play together. Helena, born in 1784, was the daughter of John Lloyd, a shoemaker of Welsh descent who had risen through his profits as a commissary in the Revolutionary War to become a New Jersey judge. She was the youngest daughter of three by her father's second wife, Antje Longstreet, the offspring of a poor Dutch family. Her mother died when Helena was seven, and she was raised by her father's third wife, who bore one child by him, Anna. Anna bought their father's farm when his third wife died in 1829, upsetting Helena, who only heard about both her stepmother's death and Anna's purchase of the farm thirdhand. Not one of her sisters or stepsisters ever wrote her in Illinois, to her great distress, though she had written to them several times.[7]

Yet despite her estrangement from her own family, she had an innate capacity for loyalty and intimate friendships from which she drew strength during the trials of the coming years. In marrying Caleb, she gained a sense of belonging to a caring, intact family. Caleb's parents, John and Elizabeth Wright Ridgway, participated actively as parents and grandparents into their late eighties, even outliving Helena and Caleb.[8] She found a great friend in Caleb's only sister, Sarah Ridgway Waln, whom she trusted completely and to whom she poured out her heart in letters from Illinois. And it was Helena who took Caleb's brother, David, into her home, just as if he were her own brother, nursing him when he was ill and almost blind[9]—but still obsessing about his mills. She and Caleb were "very happy" together, Helena wrote Sarah Waln. Rebecca, wife of Jacob Ridgway and much older than Sarah, wrote her niece from Paris where her husband was doing business, that she was glad to hear the news.[10] Yet Caleb's and Helena's "happiness" would be sorely tested in Illinois after the honeymoon period. In future years her letters indicate that Helena was able to forgive Caleb when his decisions hurt her, just as she readily admitted her own mistakes in judgment that added to his worries.

Jean Grant, who possessed maternal instincts similar to Sarah Waln's, became the object of Helena's steadfast affection almost as soon as she met her. So they had the benefit of this friendship when the families' wagons left Philadelphia. Soon they pulled onto the turnpike to Lancaster and found themselves "in the very stream of emigration. . . . Old America seemed [to be] breaking up and moving westward." They were "seldom out of sight . . . of family groups before and behind," in Birkbeck's words.[11] This first day, they would cover sixty miles because of the excellent gravel road, which had been built for the Lancaster famers who brought their produce to the Philadelphia market. Along the way, their horses would have become exhausted from pulling such heavy wagons and would have had to be exchanged for fresh ones, so liveries and taverns were frequent along the pike, promising not only fresh horses but a warm fire and hearty food—if not clean and private beds. At one such tavern on the way to Lancaster, Thomas Cope, the Quaker Philadelphia merchant, enjoyed a meal of "boiled beef, mutton steaks, turnips, potatoes, beets, cucumber pickles, preserved peaches, Indian pudding, rye bread, light sweet wheaten cakes, butter, cheese & honey, and green tea sweetened with maple sugar"—all items produced locally, none of it from the West or East Indies, except the tea.[12]

In the next day or two, they arrived in Harrisburg, where the tidy farms of the Germans—the bread basket of America and Europe—lay spread out before them. Harrisburg was the last town before they would start to cross the Appalachians, an extension of the southern mountain chain into Pennsylvania—a difficult, one-hundred mile stretch of parallel ridges and valleys. Not until the 1790s had European land-hungry emigrants ventured across, risking deadly skirmishes with hostile Natives waiting on the far side.

It is likely that the Grant-Ridgway party would have found many of their experiences of this mountainous region similar to those of diarist Thomas Lippincott, a young Congregationalist minister and merchant-clerk in Philadelphia.[13] He, his wife and their fifteen-week-old baby had left in the late fall a year earlier. Despite the rigors of the journey, Lippincott was often able to find the humor in unpleasant situations. Stopping at a tavern after a bone-shaking day in their one-horse wagon, they were "initiated into the ancient and no doubt respectable custom of sleeping *under* the bed," because the bedding was so filthy and bug-ridden. Surely the Grants and Ridgways were able to lighten their travails with laughter sometimes, too.

In Harrisburg, the Lippincotts loaded their wagon onto a flat boat to cross the Susquehanna River, and a little further on crossed the Juniata by a chain bridge. But beyond Harrisburg, the "roads [became] worse and worse." They had just started up a ridge when the "hinder axle-tree" broke and they "made their way on foot to find shelter at Henry Darr's." Held up the next day by a "very cold storm—sleet and rain," they didn't start out until the following one to climb the Alleghenies—"sloughs near miring several times." On November 20th, still in the Alleghenies, they found themselves at the foot of "dreaded Laurel Hill," with "the mud becoming very deep and frozen." The road up was "much easier than expected," while the west side was much worse. On November 21st they waded through mud for six miles on a track "much cut by heavy wagons," passing through Greenburg to arrive in Pittsburgh on November 22nd. Noted Lippincott, "We find . . . the season is so far advanced as to make it difficult to get passage" down the Ohio River.

Pittsburgh—the starting point of all journeys west—lay deep in a valley on a triangle of land where the Allegheny and Monongahela

Rivers joined to form the Ohio River. James Audubon, the famous painter of birds, and his wife, Lucy, on their honeymoon in 1803, followed the same route to Pittsburgh—the only one then—as the Lippincott and Grant-Ridgway parties did, but in a coach-and-four in April, as leaf buds were opening. They had enjoyed themselves immensely until then but found Pittsburgh in a dismal cloud, with "high mountains on all sides" keeping it always in a fog, as Lucy wrote her sister. It "is almost constant over the town; which is rendered still more disagreeable by the dust from a dirty sort of coal that is universally burnt"[14] to make glass, iron, and steam engines. It is "the blackest looking place I ever saw." Reverend Timothy Flint, a Congregational minister waiting in the town for a boat, wrote that Pittsburgh's soul was blacker than black, growing fat "on the spoils of the poor emigrants that swarmed to this place."[15]

Boats built in Pittsburgh on demand varied from slender keel boats to wide, flat-bottomed broadhorns, also known as Kentucky flats, that carried from twenty to seventy tons and had separate apartments. These flats were used by families to transport cattle, hogs, horses and household belongings. Lewis and Clark, travelling in 1804, designed their own boat for their explorations in the far west, a large dugout, or pirogue, which took weeks to be built because of delays caused by the carpenters' drunken bouts. Whisky was the bane of the Ohio Valley.[16]

After a wait of eight days, the Lippincott family finally left Pittsburgh on December 1st. The thousand-mile course of the Ohio River took some twenty to thirty days to traverse in inclement weather—if one could do it at all. Thomas Lippincott's broadhorn carried twenty-five people, with scarcely ten square feet to mingle in waking hours. It was "superlatively uncomfortable, by reason not only of the crowd, the freight and the smoke" but because of the company—"drinking sailors, profane young men, vulgar old men and women." They had to sleep six persons to a bed. Without a pilot acquainted with the river, and "owing to the low state of water," Lippincott and other responsible men had to take turns rowing, as well as standing watch all night, looking out for boulders and sandbars. At one point, he wrote, "have not slept for 42 hours."

High winds kept them off the river on some days, while on others it was only "by hard pulling" that they "contrived to keep moving." On December 4th, they encountered floating ice through which they could only make an opening "with the assistance of some people on rafts which were banded [together]." They made only six miles that day: "the prospect is gloomy." Then the baby caught "kine-pox" (chicken pox), fortunately not the "bilious fever" endemic to the Ohio Valley. "Weather getting colder and ice still running . . . fatigued and almost worn out." Finally the sun came out on December 9th, and Lippincott noticed "this beautiful river" and "ice much diminished." They passed Steubenville, which appeared to be thriving, with many log cabins, and then passed Charleston in a fog. At Cincinnati, an "elegant town" (which meant full of business, not of elegant buildings and roads, in the puzzling expression of the day), the incessant winds died down, and they passed one night in "smoothly gliding."

The falls of the Ohio River at Louisville, seven hundred miles from Pittsburgh, were a prodigious challenge in low water. The churning river dropped twenty-two feet in two miles and "was much rougher than I supposed." Thanks to a pilot, they passed over safely, but the boat leaked; Lippincott was "wet to the skin" and "the females and children in disagreeable condition."

John Melish, the Scottish cartographer, thought the falls could be described more accurately as "rapids . . . which are occasioned by a ledge of rocks, which stretches quite across the river, and through which it has forced a passage by several channels." In high water, which in spring could reach forty to sixty feet in depth, boats with a deep draught could pass over safely. But Melish passed in mid-September, when the "water [was] very low" and all the passages through them were "attended with danger." Of course, his boat had the sense to take on a pilot, and he crossed in safety, but he saw a boat strike "on the rocks, and lay there a wreck." A very practical man, he wondered, "Why is not a canal cut" around the falls to "remove the only obstacle to the trade of this fine river?" Like the medical profession at the time, he thought that "the fever and ague that sometimes prevails in the fall" was caused by winds wafting "marsh effluvia."[17]

The Lippincotts arrived in Shawneetown, Illinois, on December 30th, where they were advised that both the roads and the river to St. Louis were impassable. They wouldn't start traveling to St. Louis, their destination until February 1818, and they would have to travel overland because the river was still frozen.

In a letter to his parents from Carmi dated July 8, 1819, John Grant described their trip in general terms, as though recalling it in more detail might make the memory too painful. "Since leaving Philadelphia, my family and I suffered much fatigue and privation. Yet it has pleased a merciful God to approve our exertions, and carried us through perils by land and perils by water, in perfect safety, a distance of one thousand three hundred and thirty miles."[18]

Newspapers at the time reported that the winter of 1818 and 1819 in the Ohio Valley had been mild. The Grants and Ridgways may not have encountered as much ice as the Lippincotts. Nonetheless, the journey was still extremely difficult, especially for the men who bore the brunt of the heavy work: driving the horses in freezing rain, dragging wagons out of muddy ditches, repairing broken axles, averting pirates' attempts to steal their horses and wagons, standing watch all night on the boat, keeping an eye out for obstacles in the water, rowing for hours against the wind in a sluggish river with no current, pulling the boat free from a sandbar, or repairing it if it were damaged from slamming into a hidden rock ledge.

Meanwhile, the women—and children, too, no doubt—found the trip mostly "very tedious," as Helena wrote in her letter from Carmi to Sarah Ridgway Waln on January 14th, 1819:

> *I am happy to inform you of our safe arrival [in Carmi] at Brother John's on Christmas day, after many hardships and dangers. Our passage down the River was very tedious owing to the extreme low-ness of the Water and strong head winds. We laid by a few hours in Cincinnati and took a little view of the Town. I visited some Cousins I have there and was very much pleased to find them in a prosperous way. It is an elegant place and apparently a place of great Business. We laid a day at Louisville waiting for a Pilot to take us over the Falls, but I did not go on shore, but some of our company was very much pleased with the Town. The Falls is a tremendous looking place. The motion of the boat made me very sick for a little while but we got over without receiving any injury. We did not stop again until we got to Shawnee Town, our landing place, on the 16th of December.*[19]

As Shawneetown came into view, Jean and Helena must have given each other discouraged looks. This couldn't be the place they'd come all this way for. Debris from a recent flood lay far up the bank. Snowmelt, they may have guessed, must have almost inundated the town—if one could call it a town. It was a most unprepossessing place, just "several taverns, a bake-house, and a few huts," one visitor wrote. A traveler trying to cross the river was annoyed at finding a long line "of waggons, horses, and passengers . . . waiting to cross the Ohio" into Kentucky.[20] Kentucky was more popular than Illinois because slavery was legal there.

Yet Shawneetown was the only entry point into the Illinois Territory from the east. The United States Land Office, one of only two in the entire state, was the reason for the town's existence. The chief occupation of its few inhabitants was the salt works, or Salines, just a few miles outside Shawneetown. A federal government possession, it was worked by African slaves, who boiled down salt at one of the largest natural deposits for miles around.[21] It appears that most people who weren't enslaved accepted the contradiction that slavery existed in the Salines even though Illinois had been admitted to the Union as a "free state" on December 3, 1818. The salt was necessary to pioneers for preserving food, and the income from sales was considerable; the government was loath to give it up.

Caleb and John heaved the flatboat onto the frozen bank at Shawneetown and proposed they all get out and investigate the new country. The women likely demurred, saying they and the children were not prepared to walk in the icy puddles, with the wind so cold and blustery. The men must have agreed the women should stay on the boat and decided they would go on ahead to find Brother John Ridgway's cabin in Carmi, forty miles distant. Grant would have particularly wanted to investigate the town to choose which lot to buy. Acting promptly to set up his store was essential.

Jean, near term for her pregnancy, was glad to stay on the boat and urged John to go off, though she may not have expected to wait so long. Three days later, "on the 19th Caleb and Grant returned with Brother John with them," according to the account Helena wrote Sarah Waln, on January 14, 1819. Jean was greatly relieved at John's return. Jean had felt no contractions, but from her discomfort she knew that her baby would come very soon. Helena surely must have run out to meet Grant on his return to tell him "Mrs. Grant was taken ill," and "Mr. Grant took a room in the Tavern." Thanking John for acting so quickly, Jean asked him to leave her alone with Helena, saying they were both very experienced, and she was sure he had much to talk over with Caleb and Brother John about how and where to buy the town lot he had tentatively selected for his store. The brothers went off to look at some land to buy, but John lingered in the tavern, praying God would bring his dear wife through safely. There is a subtle suggestion in the above-mentioned letter that Helena may have been the mid-wife. As a close friend and the only woman in the group and likely in the whole town, it would have been natural. Indeed, Helena might have been returning Jean's favor of assisting her with Emma's birth in February of that year in Philadelphia.

Helena and Jean would have bought clean linen and flannel cloth in Pittsburgh and Cincinnati, preparing for this moment. Gathering the cloths together, they followed the tavern keeper to the room. He lit a candle, started a fire and promised to bring a tub of warm water from the kitchen right away. No sooner had he delivered the tin pan and Helena laid out the linens on the bed than Jean lain down, moan-ing. She made a piercing cry, alerting Helena that time was short. Helena, at the foot of the bed, saw the baby's head begin to show and then emerge so quickly she couldn't believe it had been only "about an hour" since the men "got back." Cradling the little body, Helena announced to the exhausted mother that she had a son. At the sound of Helena's "thwack" and a shrill cry, Jean surely rejoiced that her baby was breathing on his own. She might have given a silent thanks to God, though she was almost too weary for even that.

With the baby objecting loudly, Helena gently sponged him, wrapped him snugly in a flannel cloth and laid him in his mother's arms. Jean asked her friend to bend closer, as she wanted to kiss her. Helena, likely, was embarrassed by the effusive thanks.

When Helena had finished cleaning the baby, Jean and the bed, she smoothed the damp hair off her patient's face, and thought she now looked "very smart,"[22] and was ready for company. She went to find John, by then very anxious. Hearing the good news from Helena, he surely thanked her profusely. Jean would never forget the joyous look on his face as he entered the room. He patted the little bundle in her arms and bent over to kiss his son and wife. They named him Seignelay, which meant "new victory," for surely God had blessed them. (The name was a recurring one in the Cuthbert family, a Saxon family of great antiquity who had been owners of the Auld Castlehill in Inverness at one time—a family from which either Jean or John may have been descended. The name came from Charles Colbert, Marquis de Seignelay, who had been born in the Auld Castlehill but had adopted France as his home. He'd also adopted the surname, Colbert, the French version of Cuthbert, and eventually he served King Louis XIV as secretary.)

Jean and John urged the others to go on to Brother John's, which they did, reaching there on Christmas Eve. The Grant family would live on the boat they travelled on until John and the young Germans built and stocked the store (remarkably, they opened it just two weeks later, on December 31st). When the boat was no longer needed as shelter, John advertised it for sale or rent. In the same letter to his parents, written seven months aftert the family's safe arrival in Shawneetown, he added a note about Seignelay's birth.

*Carmi, Illinois, 8 July 1819*

*My Very dear, and Respected Parents,*

*. . . A few days after we arrived in this country, Mrs. Grant was safely delivered of a son—our family now consists of nine children. Six girls and three boys, blessed be God, all are as yet promising—I plead for them that they may be made the children of the most high God through the adoption of grace.*

*Adieu Adieu Adieu My dear parents — Mrs. Grant and all the dear children*

*Unite in love to you — I remain sincerely,*

*John Grant[23]*

His father, Alexander, never read this letter or the one of September 27th 1818, He had died n March 30, 1818.[24]

# 7

## THE BILIOUS DISEASE

JEAN AND JOHN SURVEYED THE STORE on the first floor of their new cabin with living quarters above. Jean laid her head on John's shoulder as he reached an arm around her slender waist. Their boots were muddy, John's gray beard and hair were unkempt, Jean's calico dress was torn and filthy at the hem, and her long hair was loose, escaped from its bonnet. They sank down onto some empty shipping crates in front of the blazing fire to survey the room. The hickory logs were spitting and crackling, fogging up the small glass panes—an unusual luxury for a first cabin.

The building was on the banks of the Little Wabash in the wooded wilderness, where the main road had only recently been cleared. None of the Ridgway brothers helped, but the Ridgway cousins, the Weeds and Wilmans, did. They already owned what had been the only store on the street, a foreign-imports store. They had been indispensable early developers of Carmi, having built a mill, distillery and store during the War of 1812. All of their efforts were spent on making a viable town, not on speculating in land.[1]

With their help and that of their indentured Germans, the Grants had erected the building, a log cabin covered in clapboard in little more than a month's time. The January thaw had helped,

as had the influx of people from a great distance offering assistance, so thrilled were they about the coming of a merchant.[2]
These early settlers had been without any manufactured goods
since arriving in Illinois, forced to improvise tools, to tan skins
for shoes, shirts and pants, and to grow flax to spin, weave and
sew into clothes.

Climbing up the stairs to their living space on the second floor,
they looked forward to sleeping in their own bedstead for the first
time in five months. They were as content as they had ever been.
After so many years of struggle to make ends meet, John and Jean
felt at last they had secured a more certain future for their family.

Their home and store were in a two-story, double-pen building, twenty-four by thirty feet, instead of the more common one-
story of twelve by fifteen feet, [3] indicating their firm commitment
to making Carmi a viable town. John had gone to bed pleased the
shelves downstairs were fully stocked and an advertisement had
been submitted to the *Illinois Immigrant* of Shawneetown: "A choice
assortment of Goods, which he has selected with care and attention
in Philadelphia and Pittsburgh, which he sells on reasonable terms
wholesale and retail." He had enlarged his inventory beyond his
fancy goods in Philadelphia. Among the new categories were tools
and building supplies (vices, spades, shovels, hoes, axes, grind-
stones for sharpening them, saws of various kinds, latches, hinges
and locks); sturdy clothing, boots and shoes; kitchen goods, such
as frying pans, pots, teakettles, Dutch ovens, sieves and cutlery;
and schoolbooks and stationery. In addition, for the few gentlepeo-
ple from the Tidewater South who had come during the territorial
period and already had permanent dwellings, John had looking
glasses, combs and glassware from Bakewell's factory in Pittsburgh.
(This was Lucy Audubon's father's factory.) He also still had the
same assortment of British cottons for wealthier customers: calicoes, ginghams, muslins, chambrays, flannels, bombazets, jaconet,

cambricks, trimmings and ribbons, and ready-made clothing, such as hose, gloves, shawls and silk handkerchiefs.[4]

◆━━━━━◆━━━━━◆

Land that been owned by Shawnees and other native tribes had been stolen piece by piece and divided by the Federal Government into thirty-six mile squares, called townships. Township 5 South of the base line, Range 9 East of the third principal meridian, Sections 13 and 14. That mouthful was Carmi's location in Egypt, as southern Illinois came to be known, because, like Egypt for the Israelites, it became the breadbasket for later settlers in northern Illinois. The government had divided land from Canada to the Gulf of Mexico and from Ohio to the Pacific into a grid of thirty-six mile squares they called townships. The Little Wabash meandered through the section where the Grants lived, from northwest to southeast. Carmi hugged both shores. Forty miles south of Carmi, the Little Wabash entered the (Big) Wabash; a few miles further, it joined the Ohio River at Shawneetown. From there, it was only a short distance to the great artery of the country, the Mississippi River, and thence to New Orleans, a ninety-day trip by barge. The steamboat, just beginning to ply these waters, promised great rewards to the early purchaser of these soil-rich bottom lands—though these early steamboats had a nasty habit of exploding.

Carmi was no more than a gash in the wilderness in December 1818, when the John Grant and Caleb Ridgway families arrived. It was "composed of log houses but improving rapidly," Helena wrote sister-in-law Sarah upon first seeing the little town "on the bank of the little Wabash." Most of it was unsettled, its population no more than fifty families. Its central "road" had been partly cleared and optimistically christened Main Street by the government-appointed officials in the territorial period, four years before, but it was rutted and muddy, obstructed by an occasional tree stump, and still wooded on its south side. Just one building stood on Main Street—a store owned by Mr. Weed and Mr. Wilmans, who had sold their earlier trading post to sell foreign imports. Elsewhere in Carmi were "six stores," according to Helena, "and a number of Mechanics of different kinds . . . All appear to have as much Business as they can do."[5]

Native Americans were not completely removed, in spite of the government's assurances. President Jefferson, as early as 1803, had enunciated the method for their removal: "When the [Natives] withdraw themselves to the culture of a small piece of land, they will perceive how useless to them are their extensive forests, and will be willing to pare them off from time to time in exchange for necessaries for their farms and families . . . To promote this . . . we shall push our trading houses, and be glad to see the good and influential individuals among them run into debt, because we observe that when these debts get beyond what the individuals can pay, they become willing to lop them off by cession of lands."[6] This appalling process was still underway when the Grants and Ridgways established themselves in Carmi.

After being disappointed in an attempt to purchase a large tract near Brother John, Hugh Weed and Frederic Wilmans, Caleb settled for eighty acres, on the east side of the Little Wabash, where flat prairie land dominated. Helena regretted that instead of being "situated within a mile of [Brother John] . . . we are going fifteen miles from them, which is a journey here." Caleb had already started "building our Cabin [and] I expect in a week or two we shall once more commence housekeeping."[7]

She hoped their cabin would be like Brother John's in time: "a very warm log house with two rooms and a Kitchen . . . as comfortably fixed" with all the "necessaries and many of the luxuries of Life."[8]

She was generally optimistic about their decision to settle in Carmi, saying she was "very much pleased with the Country thus far.

I think there is nothing but industry and frugality required to do well. The land is far superior to any I ever saw . . . There are many privations but a very great many advantages." Among the latter was the steamboat. "If you would see the superb Steam Boats on the Ohio," she wrote Sarah, "you would be tempted to visit us soon."[9]

One drawback for Helena was the lack of churches. "They have not as yet any places of worship, there is frequently Methodist and Presbyterian Missionaries that Preach in private houses . . . but their houses will not admit of many hearers . . . I hope it will not be long before we shall be blessed with many comforts that we are now deprived of." [10] Though Helena was probably Dutch Reformed, Methodist or Presbyterian preachers would likely have been satisfactory to her—that is, before she lost faith in God as her suffering increased. (Neither Brother John nor Caleb were ever known to complain of the absence of Quaker meetings.) Helena's untested faith was still intact at this early point: "I hope and trust He who has supported me through many trials will enable me to submit with patient resignation to his Divine will." [11]

The Ridgways and Grants lost contact after their move, partly because the Grants were on the west side of the Little Wabash, Caleb and Helena on the east, and Brother John's family fifteen miles to the west. Nevertheless, Helena must have visited John's store from time to time, and by June of 1819 had seen that his shelves were empty. In a June 23, 1819 letter, she wrote to Sarah Waln (who must have met John Grant) that "John Grant expects to start in a few weeks for Philadelphia."[12]

Indeed, there was such a demand for his wares that he had to head back to Philadelphia for more. Success as a merchant, which had so eluded him in Philadelphia due to restrictions on trade with Europe, must have seemed a certainty in Carmi. Optimism brimmed in this letter to his parents in July, just six months after his arrival:

*Carmi, Illinois 8 July 1819*

*My Very dear, and Respected Parents,*
*[Illinois] is a newly settled state, and very much a Wilderness A few*
*years ago, it was occupied by Savages, and now people are flocking*
*from every country in Europe and from the old States of this same*
*country—~ The land is rich and fertile and what makes it so desire-*
*able is immense tracts can be had without wood, Stones or any incum-*
*berance as soon as the purchase is done they may plough and sow it—*
*and this fine land can be bought of the Government at the low price of*
*9/ Ster^g or two dollars per Acre—a fourth paid when bought, a fourth*
*at the end of two years and then every year a fourth till paid—a tract*
*of 160 Acres what is called a quarter section—is the smallest quan-*
*tity that the Government will sell—but one man may purchase that*
*extent and sell in as small lots as may be wanted—All the unsold land*
*which is very considerable is a common for all and large flocks of cattle*
*horses and hogs are raised without any expenses. A number of the set-*
*tlers here, and from Kentucky are descendants of Scots highlanders . .*
*. Any person disposed to leave Scotland for the United States, ought to*
*come to this State—the land is low and produce is high—the settlers*
*here are thriving.*

   *I brought goods with me from Philad^a and keep store as usual*
*business has been very good only when I am run out, I am far from*
*the fountainhead.[13]*

Morris Birkbeck had warned would-be-settlers about the health risks
of living in the low bottom land—and the Grants and Ridgways
knew of the Englishman's books.[13] But settlers needed convenient
access to water, so Birkbeck's words fell on deaf ears. The settlers had
many names for the sickness that plagued the damp valleys—shakes
and aches, fever and chills, ague and bilious disease —but they had
no idea the cause was mosquito-borne malaria.[14]

John Grant, Brother John and Caleb ignored the warning and built by water. "I am fearful [the Country] is not healthy," Helena wrote Sarah not long after arriving. "My dear little Baby" Emma has "a violent Bowel complaint, a complaint that is very prevalent in this Country." She took some comfort from the words of her sister-in-law, Rebecca Ridgway: We must just have "a seasoning" (live through a few fall seasons) and we will then be healthy. Indeed, Rebecca Bacon Olden, a school mate of Sarah Ridgway Waln] herself, Brother John's wife, was evidence. "I never saw [her] look better."[15]

Having survived the summer of 1819, the Grants and Ridgways thought themselves seasoned and unlikely to become ill with the fever. But the fever hit Carmi with virulence in the summer of 1820. On August 26th the *Illinois Gazetter* announced tragic news:

*The town of Carmi has suffered by a serious and most alarming visitation. Its little population has been prostrated, or dispersed, by a violent bilious disease, which has raged among them producing in many cases the most rapid dissolution . . . The rest of White County is reported to be healthy . . . Until lately Carmi was healthy also—but 'in the midst of life we are in death'—and this flourishing village now presents a melancholy proof of the uncertainty of life. Among the victims are Mrs. Ridgeway, wife of Mr. John Ridgeway, lately of Philadelphia—an amiable and accomplished woman, who has thus been cut off in the prime of her life usefulness, leaving a small family of young children; and Mr. John Grant and his wife, who expired nearly about the same time. Mr. Grant was a native of Scotland, who removed to this state about a year ago, with a large family of children, who are now left in a land of strangers, without a relative, or a friend, except the few acquired during so short a residence. Mr. Grant was an active and useful man; and we believe a most honest worthy man. Both himself and his wife were pious Christians, in communion with their church and were exemplary for the unassuming correctness of their lives, and the kindness and cheerfulness of their hearts and manners. They have left a good name and an excellent example behind them, which their children may reflect on with pride and profit, and which encourages a hope that they have gone to a better world.[16]*

Only eighteen months after John Grant and his family had arrived in Carmi, he and his wife, Jean, were both dead. And Brother John Ridgway had lost his wife, Rebecca. Readers in Illinois, Philadelphia, New Jersey and Inverness, Scotland were stunned and grief-stricken when they read the news.

John and Jean Grant (and little Catherine and Janet, never mentioned again in letters, must have died at about the same time) were buried in the Old Graveyard in Carmi, on a bluff overlooking the Little Wabash River, south of Main Street. The wooden markers in the graveyard have long since disappeared, but in the town, a Grant Street near the site of John's store bears silent witness to the family's short sojourn there.

# 8

## "LEFT IN A LAND OF STRANGERS"

WHAT COULD THE CHILDREN HAVE FELT at the sudden loss of their parents? Perhaps the oldest, Mary, sat in the darkness, staring numbly around the front room of her father's store in Carmi. Her parents had drawn their last breaths a short while before. She was barely past eighteen, with eight younger brothers and sisters, who were asleep now in the other room. She didn't know how they were going to survive.

Distraught, she scanned the primitive and dismal front room. Though clapboards gave the outside of the cabin a finished look, inside, it felt crude and temporary. The daubing in the chinks between the logs constantly had to be repaired to keep the wind and rain out. She might have worried that a drunk or angry Native American could break the windows or door at night and kill them all. She had heard of such incidents. Her father had kept his rifle resting on cleats over the door for just such an emergency.

As her eye wandered to the outside darkness, she saw nothing but trees, their towering canopies obscuring the night sky, their trunks so thick the forest looked impenetrable. Only in the east, over the river, did she see a few stars peeking through the thicket of bamboo-like canes lining the marshy banks. She started sobbing.

Unable to see God's heaven, maybe she thought God couldn't see her, either.

Recovering her composure, she started to think of how her parents' illness had begun just the night before. Their high fever had been the first sign. She must have. tried to assuage the fever, squeezing cool water from a piece of wet cotton onto their parched lips and tongues. Then, in a few hours, they had begun shivering, as though it were not August, but winter She had piled more and more blankets on them.

Dr. Shannon[1] had come over then, likely having heard from her father's indentured German servants that her parents were ill. He was an esteemed neighbor and Mary named one of her sons after the doctor. Having seen the sickness too often before, he said their shakes and aches, fevers and chills were all symptoms of the bilious fever, common in August near marshy creeks and riverbanks in Illinois. Sadly, he said, there was little he could do, but sometimes patients recovered by themselves. (Because the symptoms were very similar to those of yellow fever, frequent in August on the Eastern seaboard, malaria was erroneously thought to be the same disease.)

Perhaps, he suggested, if one of the children were wakened and brought to their parents' bedside, the sight of him or her might strengthen their will to live. And so Mary carried in two-year-old Seignelay and lifted him, sleepy-eyed and serious, for her parents to see. But not even his plump little body had changed the vacant looks in their eyes. His parents' seeming indifference so upset Seignelay that it was only with a great deal of effort that Mary had been able to calm him.

Convinced then that death was near, Dr. Shannon had given her parents laudanum to ease their distress, the usual antidote. Mary must have been glad to see their faces relax, but she had been unprepared to see their eyes become glassy and unseeing and their hands unresponsive to the pressure of hers. And then they drew their last fitful breaths almost simultaneously. She wailed and pounded her fists on the mattress in anger. At last she had quieted herself with Dr. Shannon's help, and he had kindly left her to sit in private by their bed holding their hands, one after the other, perhaps until there was no warmth left in them. Before he'd left, Mary had asked him how she might present the deaths to her siblings. He may well have suggested she tell them—though it might seem like their father and mother had left their children—they would be watching over them every minute from heaven and would always love each of them. If the children wanted to see their parents' bodies and say goodbye, he suggested that she should let them. Finally, he added that some men would be over in a while to take away her parents' bodies and build them coffins. Mary wouldn't have known what to do without Dr. Shannon.

She may have lit some candles around her parents' bedstead so her siblings could see, and then wakened them. They came in and looked, surely only able to withstand the sight briefly, and barely able to see through their tears.

When they were all back in bed, Mary tried to lie down herself, but she was so hot and uncomfortable from her nightgown clinging to her body that she had gone to the window to cool herself. The night air was heavy and damp. Nothing was stirring. Not the air with its constant fetid smell of the marsh. Not a footstep below on the plank walkway, or a ripple of water against the bank. No furtive flight of a swallow under the eave nor the stealthy creeping of a panther, bear or wolf through a forest opening, seeking to grasp some hapless sheep or chicken. Perhaps it was always hot and quiet like that. When a knock sounded on the door, Mary almost didn't hear it; her mind was so thoroughly absorbed. She got up and let the men in. Not wanting to watch them removing her parents' bodies, she returned to her window seat.

Incidents from the past must have surfaced in her mind. She'd never been awake all night before. She remembered waking in the early morning hours to see her father standing on the steps with his rifle in his hands, but he'd stood there only for a moment. He'd thought he'd heard drunken Natives nearby. His lack of alarm had reassured her, and she'd gone back to sleep. And another time during the night, she'd heard her father fire a gun close by. When he'd come back upstairs— saying a bear had been nosing around the barn but he was gone— his composure may have relieved her, and likely a few moments later, she had been asleep again. Those were the only two times she could remember waking at all at night. She thought there was really nothing her father hadn't been able to do: shoe a horse, drop a deer in one shot and even fell a tree so it landed just where he'd planned.

Alexander, her younger brother, fifteen, had started to shave the soft fuzz over his lip and under his chin, but he was thin and his health delicate. No amount of food seemed to strengthen him or keep the sharp angles of his shoulder blades from poking through his clothing. She knew she had better prepare herself to take on the heavy work that her father had done. Though she was barely past childhood herself, and had her "follies," as her father had written his parents, "those who [were] acquainted with her wonder[ed] at her experience and sense."[2] She must have been able to do the usual farm chores: milk a cow and deliver calves, ride a horse, and handle an axe. There was no reason, she thought, not to learn to shoot a gun.

When morning came, she was still seated at the window, staring. Her eyes were burning. She must not have drifted off all night. But she couldn't account for the hours; they were lost.

The first light was wan and anemic, but as she turned to look over the river, the sky was beginning to flush with color. And beyond the bluff and down the bank, she saw Weed's and Wilmans' former mill and Hargrave's trading post coming to life.[3] Lines of people had formed with carts of corn to be ground; others carried pelts to trade for guns and gunpowder, calico, corn, venison, hams, liquor or coffee. She had waited in line there herself for corn meal. And as she sat before the window, she may have recalled not so much the unpleasant odor of the swampy river edge during her wait there, but the dazzling wings of the dragonflies hovering over the grasses. Looking through the cane-brake to the Little Wabash, she may have seen Tom, Mr. Graham's slave,[4] poling his ferry with a load of squirming hogs, already halfway to the other side, where Caleb and Helena Ridgway lived.

With these signs of life now stirring, her terror of the future must have diminished some, and she was reminded of how many things she had to do as the person everyone depended on. Her younger brothers and sisters needed her, especially three-year old Catherine and sev-en-year old Janet, both ailing, she thought, from the same malady as their parents. They were constantly fluctuating between fever and chills.[5] She would have had to think about the store opening too.

The memory of her mother repeatedly gathering strength to face daunting circumstances empowered Mary. She rose from her chair, slipped on her calico dress and, barefoot, made her way carefully across the splintery puncheon floor and out to the pump to get water. Taking some to Catherine and Janet in their beds, she urged them to drink a sip to moisten their mouths, then sponged their fever-ish skin with cool, damp cloths. While changing their bedclothes and bedding and smoothing fresh sheets over them, she may have kissed them on their necks, their cheeks, their burning foreheads, and promised she'd be back after breakfast, when she'd have time to sit and read to them. They moaned softly in reply.

Fortunately, Alexander (fifteen), Hectorina (thirteen), Rachel Magdalene (eleven), John (nine), Jane (four), and Seignelay (two), were still healthy. Mary asked their help to get the day started. They willingly responded; milking the cow, tending to the calves, horse, heifers, pigs and chickens, emptying the chamber pots, lighting a fire, putting hominy and bacon in the skillet to fry and setting the table.

As they sat down to eat, Mary asked Alexander to say a blessing such as their father might have given. No, he would not, could not, he might have said. Without showing any disapproval, perhaps in part because she, too, found it beyond her capacity to feel grateful, Mary suggested that they hum "Old Hundred," a favorite hymn of Presbyterians and often used as a blessing. That might be gratitude enough in God's eyes, under the circumstances.

Struggling to keep up the schedule her mother had set in place, Mary started the older children on their lessons. She encouraged Alexander to write an obituary for their father and ride it down to the newspaper, the *Illinois Gazette*, where he had started apprenticing for a lawyer and printer, Mr. Henry Eddy.[6] Eddy had been born to English parents in Vermont and educated in the East; he'd studied law in Pittsburgh and planned to spend his useful years helping citizens coalesce into just and effective communities through the publication of his *Gazette* and his law practice. He had floated the heavy metal letter press down the Ohio River and established the newspaper with another businessman in 1818, making it the second one in Illinois. An acquaintance recalled that Eddy was one of the most distinguished legal minds of the day in southern Illinois, often appearing before the Supreme Court: "He was employed in the largest cases that came up from Southern Illinois. When he addressed the court, he elicited the most profound attention." He was "a sort of walking law library. He never forgot anything that he ever knew, no matter whether it was law, poetry or *belles lettres*." When he was in a genial mood, he would quote long passages from Milton or Shakespeare.

Mary knew she must not put off telling the indentured Germans that her parents had died, though she dreaded it. They offered their deepest condolences and, to her relief, didn't ask what the future held for them. They passed on a rumor that Mr. John Ridgway's wife had died the day before, as well, and that almost all of Carmi was under siege from the fever, while, oddly, the rest of White County was healthy.

Sometime later, Mary and Alexander read a copy of the August 26th issue of the *Illinois Gazette* in which they quickly found their parents' obituaries. Mary and Alexander likely passed the paper from one to the other, as they sat at the long family table eating breakfast. Reading the obituary revived their grief with devastating force, and each sat silently, absorbed in private thoughts. Alexander scooped some honey onto his hominy and then some cream, still warm from the cow Hectorina had milked earlier; then he aimlessly stirred it about in his bowl without eating any. Mary got up from the table and started sweeping some inconsequential dirt, likely choosing busyness to deal with her grief.

Alexander may have broken the silence at last, and Mary went back to the table to listen. Since he was working in Mr. Eddy's office, he'd brought up the question of what the future held for their family of young orphans. Alexander must look to see whether their father left a will, the lawyer said, in which he would have named an executor and possibly a guardian for the children. It was not unusual in Illinois for a man to die without a will, however. If their father hadn't made one, the Court of Commissioners of White County would have to appoint an administrator and possibly several guardians because the family was so large. They might not be able to stay together, Mr. Eddy added with hesitation, not wanting to upset Alexander.[8] Since he and his sister, Mary, were both past fourteen years of age, he continued, they would not have to live with a guardian and would receive their portion from their father's estate right away. The younger children would have to wait until they were fourteen for theirs—if anything were left after the guardians had used it for the orphans' support and education, as the law required.[7]

Likely shocking Mary with each revelation, Alexander delivered his last bit of news as gently as he could: he had looked everywhere and couldn't find a will. Mr. Eddy said that, if this were the case, they must go to the clerk of the court commissioners, who handled the probates of intestates, to discuss their options. Mary was astonished by her younger brother's grasp of legal terms and asked him what intestate and probate meant.

Very soon, Mary and Alexander must have made a visit to the clerk. An enslaved black person answered the door and led Mary and Alexander down a hallway and then down some steps to Mr. Ratcliff's office. The clerk of the court commissioners was carrying on his work in Mr. Hay's log cabin on the river bank near the mill, until the new courthouse could be built. Mr. Ratcliff told them that he had very little power except to relay the decisions of the three commissioners, but he hastened to assure them that the law considered the commissioners financially liable if the administration of an estate were mismanaged in any way.

The clerk then took them by complete surprise with the revelation that the Grant children needn't worry about being separated: widower John Ridgway (Brother John) had petitioned the court to be named the administrator of their father's estate. If his petition were accepted by the judges, Mr. Ridgway would also become the orphans' guardian.

So much about their lives had changed so dramatically in the last few days, Mary and Alexander sat there stunned. They had only met this man once, when they'd first arrived in Shawneetown, after their family had travelled with John's brother, Caleb, and his family from Philadelphia. Walking back up the hill to their cabin on Main Street, Alexander said Mr. Ridgway's petition sounded very irregular to him, even self-serving, and wondered what his motives were. Volunteering to take in orphans was an unusual occurrence; their care and support was an expensive burden for any family. Mary only half-listened to Alexander; she was concentrating on the good news—their family would remain together.

Some days later, Mary and Alexander learned the court had accepted Mr. Ridgway's petition. Furthermore, they could see from the formal "Letters of Administration" Mr. Ratcliff had said that Mr. Ridgway had posted a $50,000 bond, required as security by the court, a precaution to prevent estates being used for personal reasons than for the orphans. When Alexander mentioned the large amount of the bond to Mr. Eddy, he was told that it usually was equal to the value of the estate. Asking how Mr. Ridgway would have known this, Mr. Eddy thought that one of the judges or the clerk knew from tax returns or land sale records. Alexander should talk to Mr. Ratcliff again, Mr. Eddy said. If their father's estate were that large, another man, someone with whom they felt comfortable, might be willing to take on its administration.

Mary and Alexander spoke for some time about several men who might be suitable administrators. One candidate was George Grant, who had been a friend of their father's. George and their father had been born just a year apart in the same county of Ross and Cromarty in Scotland. George and his brother, Colin Grant, had come to America early enough to enlist in the Continental Army. The bankrupt federal government paid them in land stolen from Native tribes, not incidentally helping populate the frontier at the same time. George had a farm in Harrison County, not far from Shawneetown by way of the Ohio River, while Colin lived in Pleasant Township, Switzerland County, Indiana, a little further east. George was sixty-one and Colin, fifty-eight. Though only George's name is known to have been suggested as an administrator, Colin may have been another of Mary's and Alexander's recommendations.

Mary steeled herself to tell Mr. Ratcliff of Alexander's and her proposal in another meeting—which this time she attended by herself. The clerk had insisted that Mary come alone, since she was the eldest, but Mary wondered if it was because Mr. Ratcliff believed she was more tractable than Alexander. She would prove him wrong. With poise and firmness, she informed Mr. Ratcliff of her recommendations. After he said he would relay her suggestions to the commissioners, she cut off any further discussion or objections by wishing him a good day and leaving.

Very soon afterward, a messenger called on Mary to bring her to another meeting with Mr. Ratcliff. When she reached his office, she saw that Mr. Ridgway was also there. The clerk introduced her to him, though she recognized him from their meeting when her family had first arrived in Shawneetown. Mr. Ratcliff went on to say that it was a great disappointment to him, but the commissioners had rejected Mary's suggestions for administrator. Refusing to be cowed, she demanded to know why every one of these men, all of whom were highly qualified, had been refused.

Perhaps Mr. Ratcliff and Mr. Ridgway ducked into an alcove to confer, their backs to Mary, whispering so she couldn't hear. After some minutes, they returned with a letter. Mr. Ridgway said it would be in her best interest to sign it. After reading the letter, she was incensed that it had been composed as though *she* had written it to the clerk. She was also half-amused because the quality of the handwriting was so inferior to hers. She refused to sign it.

Again the men may have retreated to their alcove, their voices raised this time. Returning after some time, they presented her with a new letter that acknowledged, in a backhand way, that Mary's recommendations for administrators were qualified (if only in her estimation), but it was still composed as though she had written it.

*Sir,*

*Since I last saw you I have had further advice upon the subject and the administrators have been recommended to me in place of those I had*

*considered sufficiently qualified therefore in place of the appointments*
*yesterday made I would wish to act as administrators*
*John Ridgway*            *George Grant*            *Caleb Ridgway*

*Mary Fraser Grant (signed in her own hand)*

Mary knew she had been ambushed, but by whom, she wasn't sure. She decided she had to sign the letter because at least one of the names she had suggested, George Grant, was now included. It was a sort of compromise, and that was some consolation to her. But there were now to be three guardians, and she wondered if her family was to be split three ways.

She likely walked home criticizing herself for being manipulated, but to her relief, Alexander praised her for insisting that one of their recommendations, George Grant, be on the list.

Very soon, a messenger delivered the revised Letters of Administration to Mary and Alexander. They expected to see the change from one to three administrators. Glancing further down on the long page, they indeed saw two names inserted above John Ridgway's. The first, Caleb Ridgway, they had expected to see. But the second was Frederick Wilmans—*not* George Grant.

They had been duped again. This time they suspected it was Mr. Ridgway's doing, because Mr. Wilmans, the third name, was a Ridgway cousin. Though he'd been a good friend of their father's, Mr. Wilmans' close relationship by marriage to John and Caleb Ridgway made him seem a member of a Ridgway cabal.

A few days later, three unctuous men—appraisers as it turned out—knocked on the door to make an inspection of the residence to inventory the "goods and chattels." Their rifling through drawers and cabinets, handling all the objects dear to their parents, felt like a violation to Mary and Alexander.

In December, another copy of the Letters of Administration

unexpectedly arrived at the Grant house—unchanged except for a new roster of men, whom Mary and Alexander did not know, guaranteeing the $50,000 bond. Mr. Eddy said, when he heard from Alexander, that Mr. Ratcliff—"Old Beaver," as he was affectionately known in town for his prodigious energy—must have discovered grounds for distrusting John Ridgway's list. Mr. Eddy explained that Mr. Ratcliff was a generous man and naturally would sympathize with the orphans. But in order to conduct the probate fairly, he'd no doubt tried to suppress his natural prejudice against Mr. Ridgway, a Quaker. It appeared that the Grant children were going to have to move into John Ridgway's house.

Quakers were stigmatized by the predominantly Scots and Scots-Irish population of southern Illinois because they refused to bear arms—an egregious fault in a violence-prone country—and hypocritically owned indentured servants while disapproving of holding slaves. Worse still, Mr. Ridgway was known to be a land speculator in a place where settlers were divided into two classes, in the parlance of the day—"town builders" and "speculators."

Eddy said he was favorably impressed by the new list of bond-holders. The original eighteen that Ridgway had pulled together were an assortment of Ridgway neighbors, none of them distinguished, one even illiterate. The town commissioners had required a more trustworthy list. The five who replaced them were men of sterling character who would keep Mr. Ridgway honest. Leonard White was a former justice of the Court of Common Pleas under the territorial government. Richard Graham was a devout Presbyterian who had known Mr. and Mrs. Grant from meeting with them on Sundays for worship in various private homes. Robert Shipley was a distinguished lawyer and justice of the peace, and Hugh Weed and Fred Wilmans were both principled men whose familial relationship with the Ridgways should not be held against them, Mr. Eddy said.

Hearing that such an honest man as Mr. Eddy approved of the new bondsmen eased Mary's mind. She now had confidence that the Grant orphans were in good hands.[9] They would oversee Mr. Ridgway's use of the funds until they became adults in the eyes of the law.

No more than a month later, after being called by Mr. Ratcliff to give her final approval to the probate of the estate, Mary turned to leave the courtroom only to find Mr. Ridgway waiting. He gently took her arm and helped her up the stairs and then along the river bank to her cabin. Though his attentiveness in the following days could have been read by an experienced woman as a prelude to marriage, Mary was shocked when he proposed. But she understood immediately the implications of a refusal. Her younger siblings would have no home. She accepted.

*Sarah Ridgway (Mrs Nicholas) Waln, 1779–1872.*
*Courtesy of Historic Walnford.*

# 9

## THE SPINNING WHEEL IS HER INSTRUMENT

ON JANUARY 4, 1821, FOUR MONTHS after her parents' death, Mary Grant was married at age eighteen to John Ridgway, then thirty-two, "agreeably to the rules of [Mary's] church," and not to John's Quaker faith. There were no Quaker meetings in Illinois.[1] Surely, Mary had envisioned a different kind of wedding by a Presbyterian minister to a younger man whom she might have had some romantic feeling for, and not a quick ceremony two sentences long by a government official with the notation on the bottom corner of the page, "anyone can authorize."[1]

John Grant's store and indentured Germans were sold. Then, or soon thereafter, Charles Wilmans, a Ridgway cousin, bought the cabin and used it for his business and residence.

John Ridgway distributed Grant's estate to himself, (with the exception of Alexander's share), because he, Ridgway, was the guardian of the younger Grant children, and the husband of the eldest; a wife could not own property. In an estate sale of the residue of her father's estate, Mary, as probate law required, had to buy back her own piano, four bedsteads, most of the thirty-three volumes of books, the family china and silver-plate teapot, teaspoons, candlesticks and tea tray, for a total of $77.55, all charged against her inheritance, which, in any event, belonged to her husband.

After her marriage, Mary and her siblings moved into John Ridgway's log cabin in a woodland at the edge of Seven Mile Prairie fifteen miles west of Carmi. Since it was a two room cabin with perhaps a loft, it must have been difficult for ten children, all grieving the loss of a mother or both parents — five in each family— to find a small spot to lay down a straw mattress. And just as difficult for Mary to get in bed with a stranger.

John had taken his two eldest children by his first wife, Rebecca Olden, ages eleven and twelve, from boarding school, saying he ceould no longer afford the tuition; his family was too large. Because he knew Mary was intelligent and well-educated, he had her home-school not only these two children but his youngest three (not to mention Mary's five younger siblings.) Suddenly in charge of the education of so many children must have been daunting for Mary.

On August 5, 1823, in the dim light of a candle Mary, bone-tired, stealing hours from sleep, found some paper from their limited supply to write a letter to her new sister-in-law, Sarah Waln.[2] "I will not commence my first letter with a string of apologies...but shall say it has been longer than first intended...When I received your very affectionate letter, I delayed answering" until the two older Ridgway children came home from boarding school. "Since then I have no particular cause to give as an excuse for my remissness excepting the charge of a numerous family...I have snatched this little interval when the children retired to rest to assure my dear Husband's Sister, if I appeared to slight her kindness & attention, my heart was not the less sensible... Their father has taken them from school which I regret very much... If the completion of [their schooling] be trusted with as incompetent a hand as I, it well be but imperfectly executed. ..I who am barely past childhood now."

It had been one and one-half years since she and her siblings had moved into the Ridgway household. Hectorina, by then sixteen, and Rachel Magdelaine Grant, fourteen, were both adults under Illinois law so they moved into their brother Alexander's house. But Mary still had James Ridgway, fourteen, a difficult child (or in Helena's words, "a poor specimen"), as well as Elizabeth Ridgway, twelve, and Rebecca Ann Ridgway, ten, who were both lovely, affectionate children. Then there were Mary Ridgway and John Grant both seven and Lydia Ridgway and Signay Grant both five. (The family varied the spelling of Signay and Madelaine  names) These last four may have played together helping Mary a little. By the time of her letter to Sarah, she had a one-year-old, Harriet, her first child with John Ridgway. Harriet may have been just walking, perhaps hitching herself from table to chair and getting into everything. But at the moment she was writing, Mary was keeping an ear out for Harriet's labored breathing. Harriet had "that ugly complaint which proves so fatal to children in Philadelphia."

The next morning, Mary's step-daughter, Elizabeth (named after her grandmother), added a note to Mary's letter. Mary had taught her to write a letter like the one she had learned at Stephen Addington's School for Ladies in Philadelphia. Mary had written, "My dear Aunt, Perhaps you may expect a more complete letter from me but I hope your affection will excuse any faults you may see in it." And Elizabeth wrote "My beloved Aunt, My letter is so childish. I hope your affection will excuse my blunders."

Elizabeth's letter is a window into the household, telling of the scarcity of money and its effect on the family. She didn't understand more than that, but the devaluation of state-chartered bank notes that had brought commerce to a halt in the East was even worse in the West. There was no monetary form of exchange. Everyone hoarded any gold and silver they had. The Western economy was reduced to barter.

"Things are so dear and there are so many of us to clothe," Elizabeth wrote. "To card and spin cotton is such tedious work, we might make two pieces flax and wool while we are making one of cotton. But the flax and wool are so scarce in this country, shirts and sheet and everything is made of cotton. As I have been to school so long I am only learning to spin. Rebecca [who had been at home] has spun half the filling [wool weft] of two pieces of cloth, one for coarse shirts, the other for frocks." Homespun and linsey-woolsey refer to the same kind of cloth—one which has a linen warp and wool weft.

Elizabeth asked her aunt to please thank Uncle Andrew for the calico. "I don't know what we would have done without it." She can barely contain her excitement about the possibility of a new bonnet or frock. Also exciting to Elizabeth was a party in a few days. Women friends like Aunt Helena and Mrs. Wilmans were to join them because a carding machine was to be brought.

At last the women would have the pleasure of company other than their family. "There is but one carding machine in this part of the country it is but a few miles hence and they have promised to come down in the waggon and bring their wool." Instead of two hand paddles with hooks to rub a mass of wool eventually turning it into fibers to be spun, a carding machine was a heavy piece of equipment. It consisted of two large drums or rollers covered with "pin cloth" or metal covers around the drums, one with large pins, and the other with small. The washed mass of wool was laid on the receiving tray. With the cranking of a handle, the drums turned and the wool was pulled in and transferred from one drum to the other repeatedly until the fiber were perfectly aligned. The "roving" was then pulled off the drum with a "doffer stick" and was ready to be spun. A great deal of wool could be processed quickly by the machine compared to the hand method. One imagines how pleasurable —and how rare——it must have been for the women to visit together, especially for Mary, the newcomer in the group.

James was supposed to write a letter to Uncle Andrew when Elizabeth had finished. She didn't think he would and she was correct. Mary must have known James was difficult by then but she believed that "when a child turns out contrary to the hopes and wishes of a parent, I think that parent has been deficient in some point or another." Mary hoped Sarah's affection for the "dear orphans entrusted to her, would incline her to be more lenient with me than a mere stranger would."[2]

Mary's second and last letter to Sarah, June 4, 1824[3] reveals a self-assured woman who has adapted to her roles as mother (by then of two children) and as wife to her husband, who clearly respected her abilities and she, his. John would be elected in 1826 to represent White County for two years at the State Legislature at Vandalia. (He would rarely be home, we learn later from Helena—a trial for Mary.) Mary wrote that she and John had made an important financial decision jointly unusual for the times. "We have taken [brother] David's mills [in bad repair on the Wabash River] with a view to better ourselves & moved up to this place. Our house is not near as comfortable, neither have we as good water, nor as nice a garden. Our family which before consisted of twenty, is enlarged by the addition of several hands, all tend to make it disagreeable. But I am willing to forego the comforts of life, for the sake of ensuring every necessary. For really I began to fear we should want many things. I never heard of such distressing times where war or famine was not the cause."

Mary began her 1824 letter with a story of a most unusual wedding. Brother David "arrived here last fall just in time to be precipitated into a vortex of misery." Sarah Wilmans, daughter of a respectable family and distant cousin, had announced before he arrived that if David would marry her "she would have him," though they had already had several failed engagements. Hectorina (Mary's sister) was to be married in a few days and that was the time Sarah wanted to marry David. "But when the company were assembled & the ceremony performed she burst into tears" and said she could not marry him because she could not love him. The next morning she wanted a divorce.

After this gossipy beginning, Mary shifted the mood dramatically to an account of their Western life with no money to buy anything or to pay anybody for help. "For we are constantly to spin. . . and having to cook & wash for so many additional [hands] from morning to night. It does seem too hard to keep . . .Rebecca at hard work [spinning] constantly when [she] could be improving so rapidly in her learning. . .Poor girl, the spinning wheel is her instrument. . .But am I not blessed with my [dear] husband & children all enjoying good health and yes the means of support and maintenance, and if I have neither the money nor time to obtain for my children those accomplishments I went with yet I still have one seventh of time [presumably on the Sabbath] to devote to their souls instructing and endowing their minds, with the knowledge of religion."[3]

Helena's daughter Elizabeth [also named after her grandmother] had written a similar account of her family's difficulties a few months before in a May 25, 1824 letter to her Aunt Sarah.

*My Dear Aunt,*
*Father & the rest have to gone to meeting. We have Meeting of some kind round us almost every day in the week [Robert Owen would soon arrive in New Harmony and meetings to prepare for his utopian commune were taking place almost every evening]. We see very hard times. [We do] nothing [but] work and we get nothing for that. . .My mother. . . she take in all the sewing and knitting she can get. She knits socks & sell them, spins cloth & exchanges it at the store for necessaries,*

*but it is very bad trade, they will not allow the worth of the cloth, they can get Factory cloth so low they say it is no profit to buy our home-spun. However we are obliged to do it.*[4]

Hope was high among Westerners that Robert Owen would eliminate all such problems when he arrived and transform relations between people into a perfect society, as they believed he had at his New Lanark Mills in Glasgow.

# 10

## AN UNEXPECTED HONOR

FOR EONS, NATIVE PEOPLES EXTRACTED salt from the "Great Salt Springs" and animals gathered to lick the salty mud in what would become Southern Illinois. African slaves were first introduced to extract salt from the licks by French explorers and fur traders and when Americans won the salt licks they introduced still more slaves.

America immediately began to remove the native tribes from their ancestral land, first buying it for a few bushels of salt annually, then promising the tribes land in northern Illinois and finally removing them altogether to Arkansas and Oklahoma. Euro-Americans were impatiently waiting to establish farms, some to grow cotton in the lowlands near the rivers bringing their slaves with them, and others to grow food crops, both types of farmers counting on sending barges to New Orleans to trade.

When Illinois was to be admitted to the Union in 1818 as a state free of slavery, a clause allowing "indenture"—the equivalent of slavery in practice—was inserted into the state constitution to allow the enslaved blacks to continue to work in the Salines, as they would until Emancipation in 1863. The state of Illinois was to become the lessee of the federal government and thus, the beneficiary of the revenue from the free labor of Africans in the Salines.

The new Illinois government chose the area, ironically named Equality by a visiting French man, as the site of the Gallatin county courthouse. It was here, that Alexander, John Grant's son, made his home as a student of law under Henry Eddy. He was admitted to the bar in 1826 at twenty-one and soon purchased Eddy's *Illinois Gazette* and printing company. He is said to have become fully engaged in the fractious debates of the 1820s in editorials for the paper, though none have survived.

Slavery was the leading issue of contention after Illinois was admitted to the Union. A great uproar arose among some Illinois residents to call a new Convention to revise the state constitution to permit slavery, though their purpose was never expressed so bluntly. Pro-conventionists were would-be cotton growers in the heavily veg-etated, malaria-infested lowlands of the Ohio and Mississippi Rivers. Because only Africans were immune to the disease, pro-convention-ists needed them to clean out the rank vegetation, establish cotton farms and then work them. The pro-conventionists were democrats who believed political power resided in the people not the elite. Known as "the People," or "White Folks," they were generally poor and often illiterate. Largely descended from Scots who had settled in the mountainous regions in Virginia, Tennessee and Kentucky, they were evangelical Presbyterians.

The distinction was never clear-cut, between the two groups, but anti-conventionists wanted no slaves in the state— unless they worked in the Salines, because Illinois by then received the reve-nue. They were variously called "Yankees," "Easterners," "Big Folks," "great constitutionalists lawyers," or "high-faluting Federalists," all derogatory terms. They lived in the more northerly parts of Southern Illinois. They raised food crops, not cotton. And they were not evan-gelical Presbyterians.

Both sides included racists. Henry Eddy, an Easterner and a judge, one of the Big Folks, feared Africans in Illinois, because they might be freed. "So many free blacks in our state [would] threaten "our wives and daughters who would be continually insulted by" having to live among them. Freed Africans would mix with whites and people would become "dark, indeed in complexion but infinitely darker in moral character."[2] Alexander would have been viewed as one of the Big Folks too and he likely had opinions similar to those of Henry Eddy. One of Mary's letters to Aunt Catherine mentions Alexander's "bound boy."

It was during this period that the Second Bank recalled gold and silver and the economy was reduced to barter. For example, one merchant advertised in the January 1st *Intelligencer* that he would receive "in exchange of goods, wheat, pork, butter, fur peltries, etc.,"[3] in his store in Carmi. And Henry Eddy, the same year bought 22 reams of paper for his *Illinois Gazette* totaling $96 in exchange for 9-1/2 dozen. deerskin at  $6 each totaling $57, receiving a note at  four months for the balance of $39 from Creamer and Spear.[4]

The depression affected all residents but particularly those who owed taxes or payments to the land office, faced foreclosures, or even starvation. This latter group "felt the fabric of society fray."[5] Political figures from the opposition were burned in effigy, mobs became violent, and murders were frequent, as were kidnappings of free Negroes. Abolitionist George Flower, partner of Morris Birkbeck, lost his son to a revenge stabbing.[6]

The vote for a Convention to revise the state constitution was held in 1824 and the pro-slavery group lost their bid in a decision complicated by vote trading and private dealing. In any case, slavery continued in Illinois until the Emancipation, though never openly acknowledged. Exhausted by so much political fervor on both sides, the people of Illinois abandoned the issue of slavery and it faded into the background.

A decade after the Convention vote, Alexander wrote a letter in 1834 to Illinois Congressman Robinson who was unwilling to vote to override President Jackson's veto of rechartering the Second Bank (established in 1816) of the U. S. Even though Alexander favored keeping the Secocnd Bank, he disagreed with the congressman on constitutional grounds: "To act upon the principle that the veto is. . .insurmountable, appears to me to be yielding still another prerogative to the mass of powers lately claimed to belong to the executive. Indeed the President of these United States, at the rate at which we are now going on in my humble opinion will soon be out of sight in advance of Louis Phillippe or William 4th." Grant thought President Jackson felt free to act against the people's will because his patronage appointmentees were indebted to him. Political parties such as Jackson had created, Alexander wrote, were not mentioned in the constitution and could destroy popular sovereignty, the heart of the constitution.[7]

Alexander's four surviving letters to his Aunt Catherine Grant in Scotland, detailing the news of the Grant family, date from 1826–1835. He marvels in each letter that though she has never seen most of them she takes an affectionate interest. In one, he writes, "You are the only one of our father's relations with whom any of us has had the least communication, and we might have looked up to you as the only survivor of those whose blood was the same as our own."[8]

Sometimes her letters arrived at just the right time. "My spirits [were] sunk, he wrote, from the sickness and death that I witness around me, from the attack of this prevailing epidemic, from which I was just essaying a recovery myself. Our little village, and indeed what we denominate the Western country, generally, have been sorely visited with . . . disease."[9]

She apparently asked why he didn't return to Scotland. He acknowledged that his decision "to allow his fortunes to grow and keep pace with the country . . . may have been mistaken . . . With all my exertions, [I] can make but a scanty living . . . The goodness, in a pecuniary point of view of this country is, I may say, of a negative kind. . . [consisting] in the cheapness of a living – such as it is." He confessed that he had little *"amos patriae."* At the same time, he believed the principles of American law were "unparalleled in the history of nations," which gave him, "a confidence of [America's] superiority. . .The People. . .in this country [are] the source of all political power."[10]

Despite a certain stiffness in his writing style, Alexander must have been amiable in person for he was popular within his circle of friends and much beloved by all his family. His home became the refuge of his younger brothers and sisters, nieces and nephews. He was very much a parental figure to the younger ones and very solicitous in planning for their future.

Alexander relayed the news of all the family to his Aunt Catherine in a letter of October 7, 1834. Mary has "six of the most interesting children I ever saw—three girls, Sarah Jane, Harriette and Eliza; and three boys, John, Thomas and George Alexander." Mary herself "has been engaged for about two years in keeping a school [and teaching piano] in a town called Shawneetown, the principal town in the county. She has, to average it, done tolerably well at it, until lately, raising by her profits, united with some means in the power of her husband, a competent support for her family." In the same letter, he also summarized the doings of his other brothers and sisters. Rachel Magdalene and Jane were living with him and "are still single, and lovely girls, of good mind—unexceptionable dispositions, and attractive appearance," he wrote to Aunt Catherine. "The former is delicate in her habit and constitution, and grave in her demeanor; Jane is a healthy-looking girl, dignified in her manner, intelligent and imaginative, tho' in no wise superior to her sister. John has become a merchant, of the adjoining state of Indiana . . . is married to a young lady whom he describes as everything that is charming, and what will probably please you most, is, with his wife, a devout member of the Presbyterian Church. At his request, I sent him near a year ago his youngest brother, Signalay, who is serving his time with a merchant of Indianapolis." Hectorina "is the mother by her first husband, Mr. Grant, of a fine, promising boy, named John, after his lamented grandfather."[11]

Hectorina and her husband settled in New Harmony, Indiana, the town Robert Owen bought from George Rapp in 1825. Jane went to the school that Owen established and both Jane and Rachel lived with Hectorina off and on from 1825-1828. It was close enough for Alexander to visit or for the girls to move back and forth.

Alexander described the school in an 1826 letter to Aunt Catherine as "founded on the principles of Pestalozzi . . . Mr. Owen's System has attracted considerable attention with us, more I dare say than it deserves. His ostensible aim, viz. the amelioration of the condition of the human species, is certainly very laudable. His great aim is considered by some doubtful—he is by far the greatest enthusiast I ever saw or heard of at present. The society appears to be doing little yet there are collected together a number of intelligent men informed men—and were he to be less refined in the minutiae of his system, more unequivocal in his answers to questions put to him, and not quite so zealous, he might possibly succeed."[12]

In answer to Aunt Catherine about Jane's education, Alexander wrote in an 1828 letter that he took "great pleasure in undeceiving you with regard to the situation of Jane—she is living with Hectorina at New Harmony, to be sure, but is not under the care, guidance nor influence of any person or institution. I believe the religious opinions of Mr. Owen, the patron, or pretended patron, of the place, are far from orthodox; but I can at the same time address you that his influence is nothing, and Jane is educated at a school similar to all others in the country, except that it may be superior—such at least was the case when I saw her last. I am going to N.H. in a few days and will prevail on her, if possible, to write you. Rachel M. is also with Hectorina, and as yet unmarried; though whether she have suitors or not, as, if any, what sort of attention she yields them, I am unapprised.[13]

At age twenty-nine, Alexander was elected to the state Supreme Court, the youngest Justice in the history of Illinois. He rode the circuit courts of the counties in Southern Illinois in all kinds of weather, fording streams on horseback, and probably contracted malaria from the exposure. He died at thirty-one.

*Shawneetown Jan. 31ˢᵗ, 1836*

*My dear Aunt,*

*With a sad heart do I now address you. Sad indeed, for the greatest trial that could possibly befall us, since the death of our beloved parents, is now sent to us—That dear, dear brother, who had been the guide, the stay, the support of the family, who had acted as a father to the younger part, and an instructor, adviser & protector to the elder part, is gone —can I write it, can I think it possible. . . he was taken from us, by one of those severe bilious attacks, which annually sweep away thousands in our country. . .all this time he had three sisters to take care of, and nearly all the time Hectorina & her son & Seignelay—John, though not much of a pecuniary burden to him, has been a source of anxiety to him, until a short time ago— For in early life, John did not promise to be the steady, upright character, he has since become, & poor Alexr, suffered a great deal of solicitude & trouble on his account.*

*I was not with him during his last illness, Jane was the only one of the family who enjoyed that inestimable privilege. I knew, he was one who would never become a Christian. He died at Vandalia, the seat of government, a considerable distance from this place. Jane & Maddie are now at Equality, at the house of Dr. Dake, Hectorina's husband—yet, his friends waited on him, nursed him with the devotion of brothers & as such they mourned him. Were Jane here she could give you a more full account than I, of his sufferings. He was taken in a week before last Christmas—& died on the 17ᵗʰ of this month. He had every kindness, every attention that man could possibly pay to man—Jane was the only relative he had. . . Dr. Dake was the physician who travelled two days and nights to go and attend upon Alexr and that through mire & swamp, when he was so lame he could scarcely walk— I send you by this opportunity a newspaper wherein his death is mentioned in a way that will testify in what estimation he was held by his fellow citizens. Not contented with mentioning it in one place, as is the general custom among us—they have spoken of it in four—Not one word of praise is there exaggerated that they have called him—I will rub the places with ink around—that you may notice them. The rest of us are well.*

*Sincerely, your affectionate niece,*
*Mary*

Mary forwarded one of several obituaries with her letter, this one from the January 22, 1836 issue of the *Gallatin Democrat and Illinois Advertiser*: "He was amiable in his disposition, courteous in his manners, generous to a fault in his nature and of characteristic disinteredness of motive. His temper naturally vivacious, made him the life of the circles of which he was a respected member . . . He was intelligent and just, and all who knew him respected him as a man, and loved him as a friend."[14]

# 11

AN ADVENTURE IN HAPPINESS

WHEN HECTORINA LEGALLY BECAME an adult at fourteen in 1821, she moved out of Mary Grant and John Ridgway's
household where she'd been since eleven, and into her brother
Alexander's home in Equality. Alexander, just two years older was
instantly transformed from a bachelor to a parent of a teenager, so
to speak (though he was only sixteen). Hectorina was lovable but
willful and hard to control. After three years with Alexander, she
married at seventeen a man so unremarkable that no one in the
family ever gave him name. From a friend, we learn he was young,
born in England, and had the last name of Grant. Alexander must
have been relieved of her care but at the same time, as the conscientious young man he was, he worried about what would become of
so young a couple. Quite a few years later, at her second marriage,
in a rare moment of self-reflection, Hectorina wrote to her Aunt
Catherine, "You will see, my dear, Aunt, that I believe in marrying."[1]

When she and her husband heard that the Scottish industrialist, Robert Owen, was offering free housing at New Harmony,
they along with eight hundred or more people moved into the one
hundred fifty houses Rapp's followers had abandoned. The majority of the new inhabitants, including Hectorina and her husband

were probably unaware of Owen's plan to use them for a utopian experiment.

Since the houses were built for celibate people and not families, people had to share space with others. Hectorina, her husband and their five-month-old daughter found themselves searching for space in their house for two sons from Thomas Pears's large family, whom Hectorina was surprised to see again after so many years. Mrs. Pears was just as startled to see Hectorina and wrote her aunt that she had "unexpectedly found an old acquaintance. You will undoubtedly recollect Hectorina Grant, the daughter of the late Mr. Grant of Carmi. She has married a young man of the same name, and has a sweet little girl five months old. She asked a great deal about your family."[2] The Pears had met Hectorina six years before when the Grant family had come through Pittsburgh on their way west to Illinois. John Grant had bought glass to sell in his Carmi store from Thomas Pears, a glass manufacturer there. Pears, unlike most of the new residents, came to New Harmony because he was captivated by Owen's idea of a world without hatred and self-interest.

When Owen initially arrived at his new community in New Harmony on April 27, 1825, Hectorina and her husband and daughter, Jane, were in the audience, seated in the big church Rapp built, when Owen gave his opening address: "I am come to this country to introduce an entire new State of society; to change it from the ignorant selfish system, which shall gradually unite all interests into one, and remove all cause for contest between individuals."[3] It sounded promising to the people assembled there. A few days later, he expanded his thoughts on the need to create the community in several steps. First a Preliminary Society had to be "formed to improve the character and condition of its members, and to prepare them to become associates in Independent Communities, having common property."[4] The common property idea puzzled some. And how could they operate without money, they wondered. Owen explained that the "Valuation Lists" would take the place of money—the hours of work would be credited to a member and applied against expenditures by that member from the community store for such things as clothing and food. The amount to be credited to the account for each family seemed inadequate to cover their basic expenses—a cause for some concern. But they liked Owen's idea of annihilating selfishness and strife between individuals. The influence of Owen on Hectorina was probably minimal. He was only there one month and she was seventeen at the time, and undoubtedly preoccupied with her first baby.

In contrast to Hectorina's probable lack of attention to Owen's speeches, Mr. Pears marveled at Owen's ability to mesmerize the crowd. Pears wrote a friend after hearing Owen, "I am then always in the hills. I do not know how it is — he is not an orator; but here he appears to have the power of managing the feelings of all at his will."[5] He recalled that after the valuation lists were explained and each family learned what its allowance was, "dissatisfaction prevailed." A day or two after, when Mr. Owen spoke again, the dissatisfaction had "vanished."[6] Pears regretted Owen's departure after only one month because he already felt divisive "party spirit" emerging. Owen had to take care of matters in Scotland but promised he'd be back in a few months.

Life on the frontier continued to be ephemeral. In a sad postscript to a letter, Pears wrote that Mr. Birkbeck had drowned crossing the Fox River returning from a meeting in New Harmony to his home in Albion, the town he had founded, just north of Carmi: "He came here three days ago in good health and today he is an inhabitant of the narrow tomb."[7] And three months later in early September, Mrs. Pears wrote, "Poor Hectorina Grant has lost her lovely child. It was the sweetest little creature that I have ever seen. It was a very severe stroke for her. I think she is a very good-hearted young woman, and that you would be much pleased with her."[8] Baby Jane was one of nine children lost that September. There was a swamp adjacent to the town. Mosquitoes breeding there carried malaria to the community, taking many lives, especially among the young.

The mood in the community deteriorated in Owen's absence, matching Hectorina's sadness and anger at losing her daughter. Manufacturing was not occurring. There was a building left by the Rappites for spinning, weaving, and sewing for the community's use in making clothes and sheeting, but Mr. Pears lamented that nothing had happened there. "Our factories did I say—it should be our cotton factory—has not, I believe, [been used] for all was out of order."[9]

People expected Owen to return in the fall of 1825, but that was not to be. Hogs ruined the garden. People were forced to buy food from nearby farms. Mosquitoes from the swampy ground were flitting everywhere. "They told us on our arrival they were to disappear the first two or three hot days."[10] They hadn't. Pears wrote, "Mr. Owen's heart, I think, ran away with his head,"[11] The Preliminary Society Owen had set up before he left became a committee of the elite. It was, said Mr. Pears, like living under "an aristocracy."[12] Mrs. Pears corrected her husband: "He ought to have called it despotism."[12] The Preliminary Society, of which Caleb Ridgway was a member, put out a number of rules and regulations, according to Owen's direction for how they should proceed in this introductory phase. Wednesday evenings were for discussions of issues relevant to the formation of the commune, Thursdays were for instrumental and vocal concerts and Fridays for a ball. Dancing was popular among the young who said at least in this way New Harmony was "quite gay."[14] Mr. Pears wrote the town needed a leader. Mrs. Pears lamented she couldn't do her assigned work of sewing because there was no cotton or thread.

When Owen finally arrived in January 1826, months after he'd promised, all was chaos. But Owen, living in his theoretical world failed to notice. Instead he praised them for all they'd accomplished.

He'd expected it would take three years. Therefore, he said, they could move on to the next step, the Permanent Community. A committee was chosen to write a constitution. After several drafts it was passed unanimously, so anxious was the community for order of some kind. But doubts still lingered about how the valuation of credits for each family could possibly meet its basic expenses. Also puzzlement prevailed about why Owen had such contempt for religion and why he "rejects the Scriptures."[15] They were experiencing so much inner confusion and paralysis that they asked him to be dictator for a year. Owen was happy to oblige as he was accustomed to ordering people around. So bells went off at 5:30 am and people worked to 6 pm with short breaks for meals, followed by lectures in the evening.

Owen had severely misjudged the hold individuality and religion had on the people. Like Mrs. Pears, Hectorina considered herself a Christian and Owen's godless views didn't change her Presbyterian heart at all. She was more worried about the safety of her unborn baby due in September than about meeting her scrubbing and cooking assignments.

Many people departed with the resultant happy consequence of less crowding in houses. Owen continued to believe everything was on course. He busied himself with designing large buildings he planned to erect around a central square, and thinking up odd costumes for people to wear—pantaloons for every day wear for everyone, and black and white striped dress for weddings. In order to keep religion out of marriage, he performed weddings himself, simply declaring unceremoniously and summarily that the couple was married.

Only two months after Owen's second arrival, Mrs. Pears wrote, "My health is now, as well as my poor baby's, extremely delicate . . .How I am to go on cooking and scrubbing I really do not know. But I know if I were to consider this world only, I would rather, far rather Mr. Owen would shoot me through the head. My mind is in such a state that I am almost incapable of doing anything. . . My health and strength have received such a shock, which they will probably never recover. . .Only in the grave can I see any prospect of rest. . .I can stand it no longer. I wish you to know things as they are in reality, and not to be deceived by the lies which they tell in the newspapers about happiness and contentment."[15] Mr. Pears, usually more sanguine, wrote, "Every object for which I came here is disappointed, and instead of endeavoring to show THE ROAD TO HAPPINESS to others, I know not how to secure my own."[16]

Mr. Owen's unpopularity was growing. He was "ever changing, never at rest,"[17] wrote Mrs. Pears. By April, bilious attacks were taking the lives of the young again. Exhausted and at their wits' end, the Pears family went back to their home in Pittsburg sometime in the spring of 1826.

Hectorina was pregnant so she and her husband couldn't pick up and leave. Their second baby, John, was born in September 1826.

A year after the Pears left, in 1827, Owen gave his Farewell Address, by then abhorred by all, but congratulating himself on his success.

Five months after Owen left, in October 1827 Hectorina had her third baby. Her sisters, Jane and Maddy, joined her family in New Harmony to help, and life began to seem normal again. However, in May 1828, Hectorina's baby died at seven months just as her first had. And about the same time, her husband died as well. The three sisters and John, a toddler by then, fled the community, moving in with their brother Alexander in Equality.

Hectorina and her young son lived with Alexander for the next six years, until in 1834 she married her second husband, a widowed physician with grown children, Arnold Dake. He was "the most eminent physician in this section of country,"[19] wrote Alexander to his Aunt Catherine in Scotland. They had one son, Alexander, named after his uncle. Dr. Dake died in 1838 after only four years of marriage. Before Hectorina was thirty-two, she had lost both parents, three siblings (all in their thirties—Alexander, Jane, and Mary Ridgway), two husbands and two babies. Of the Grant children who lived in the area around Shawneetown, only Hectorina and Maddy remained and soon Maddy died too. Of course, Hectorina had the care and company of her two sons, John Grant, twelve, and Alexander Dake, one. The two boys remained close throughout their lives, living in the same household in Alabama[20] when they were young men and later started a construction business together, erecting buildings around Chilton County, Alabama, one of them the county courthouse.[21]

# 12

As She Lived So She Died—A
Humble Christian

Even with the company of her two boys, Hectorina wished she had a husband. So when an attractive man of many accomplishments and charms got off the steamboat from New Orleans in Shawneetown in early July 1842, she married him two weeks later on July 20.[1] He said his name was Juan Honfleur and she had no reason to doubt him. If Alexander had been alive, he would have steered her away from Juan. But the guardian of his younger impulsive sister was gone.

Since Juan's haunts were the eastern seaboard cities and the Old South, it seems unusual that he would go to frontier towns like Carmii and Equality to set up another of his art classes. He must have heard of a desirable widow there.

He was an imposter—and  Hectorina wasn't the first to be deceived by him. Stories about him surfaced in newspapers across the country in 1838-39.[2] He had seduced at least two women previously. The first was Mrs. King, his pupil in an art class he ran in England with his wife, Mrs. Holland. Juan and this young pupil, Mrs. King, fled to America, where they started an art school like the previous one in England and changed their names to Mr. and Mrs. Juan Honfleur. They taught classes in various cities, moving periodically between Boston, Macon, Charleston and Nashville. In 1838, they were located in Lexington, Kentucky.[3]

There, this "man of distinguished personal attractions"[4] met his next victim: Susan Rodgers. Originally from Philadelphia, she was an assistant music teacher in the school and lived in a "genteel mansion." But she was "withal a very ugly girl."[5]

In newspapers the tale of Susan and Juan was usually titled "The Elopement." Under secret of darkness, "the gallant Lothario" took Susan to Cincinnati on a steamer in May 1838.

Demonstrating that she was a woman of independent means, her extravagance likely not lost on Juan, she ordered her trunks to be taken aboard, and "with a Cleopatran air, seized a pen and drew an order on her agent in Lexington for $20." Within a month, Susan must have left him, for he was reported to have no money in June 1838: "The Arch Fiend" and "smooth-face villain . . . with an oily tongue and impudence . . . has since been cast adrift in a town in the west, where it is said 'he is moneyless, shirtless, coatless, and for a while longer gallowsless.'"[6]

In April 1839, three years before he married Hectorina, he was arraigned for bigamy." He claimed his only legal marriage in the U. S. was to Susan in Ohio, and he pulled a marriage certificate from his pocket, surprising even his lawyer. Furthermore, he said, he was never married to his partner in the art school in Lexington, though she was known as Mrs. Honfleur. His only other marriage was to a Mrs. Holland, daughter of an engraver, in England. Because it took place in a "foreign country," he was "not liable to punishment for the bigamy and the indictment  was quashed  A few months later, on September 12, 1839, Susan, "wife of Juan Honfleur" was dead.[7]

Whether Hectorina and Juan moved from city to city teaching art classes as was his custom or settled in one isn't known but in 1850, they were living in Nashville.[8] This was a city of many cultural attractions, a university, theater, music—the kind of city Juan liked. Hectorina enjoyed it too, walking her boys there was so much more interesting than in Shawneetown.

In 1850, Hectorina learned that a William Robertson and his wife Ann Fraser were living in St. Augustine, Florida. William may have been related to Aunt Robertson in Scotland with whom she and Mary had corresponded. Ann was born in Inverness, married William Robertson, a draper there, (cloth merchant) and in 1818 moved to St. Augustine.[9]

Hectorina became preoccupied with meeting the Robertsons. She pleaded with Juan to take her to St. Augustine after he finished his classes in Nashville and he agreed.

To prepare for the journey Juan began studying maps, train and stage schedules to supplement his own extensive travel experiences. The challenge was to reach some transportation hub. He had already been following newspaper reports of the furious and successful pace of railroad building across the south in order to transport cotton quickly ro British mills. One rail line ran from the southwestern cotton-growing lowlands of Alabama; the other from the northwest Georgia and Tennesse mountain valleys where short staple cotton thrived. These two rail lines, from the south and north, carried the cotton bales to Chattanooga where, after 1850, they were loaded on a train to the Atlantic ports and from there to the Manchester mills. Though the rails were built expressly to get the cotton to Britain as quickly as possible, they served passengers as well.

The absence of any rail from Nashville to Chattanooga (called Ross's Landing by locals), posed a dilemma for Juan—whether to take a circuitous steamboat route on the Tennessee River from Nashville to Chattanooga, or whether to go by stage coach up and across the

Cumberland plateau fourteen hundred feet above Nashville.

Finally Juan decided on the stage. He told Hectorinna that by April the shoals on the Tennessee River would be too dry to cross over. Water levels were highest in December.

But Hectorina had heard frightening stories of stage coach accidents. Stages crossing flooded creeks could pose problems for horses. If a horse fell, the carriage, passengers and baggage could be washed downstream, causing many fatalities; or a stage coach could contain undesirable or drunk companions; it could pitch too far one way and that and if the driver's commands to lean to the other side were ineffective, the coach could fall over; the horses could be mired in mud up to their knees; or the horses could tire of pulling a heavy coach up a steep grade and refuse to go further.

The day of their journey arrived and Hectorina and Juan waited stoically for the stage. Her two boys were twenty-four and fourteen and would have set up their own household together by then. Hectorina pointed to a warning she saw carved into a beech tree: "Hell is one mile from here,"[10] and her fears were rekindled. Juan tried to stiffen her resolve stressing the reward of seeing the Robertsons. Once loaded, the stage began the arduous trip up the road which required countless switch backs to render the grade one with which the horses could contend as they labored up the mountain. Finally reaching the plateau the horses encountered more difficulties crossing the many streams.

Twenty two hours later the Honfleurs arrived in the quiet town of Ross's Landing—or Chattanooga—wilted and aching. Uncurling their bodies from the crowded coach, they climbed stiffly down to the ground. This had been land belonging to the Cherokee Nation only a few years before. John Ross, who was part Indian and part Scot, and later Chief of the Cherokee Nation, had operated a popular trading post and ferry on the Tennessee River. He, along with other Cherokees, had been forced to leave after the Cherokees lost a war to American troops in 1835. Three years later, under the Indian Removal Act, federal emigration officials rounded them up and forced them down the steps of Ross's Landing onto boats to travel from there to the western side of thee Mississippi River to Arkasas or Oklahoma, a journey that came to be known as the Trail of Tears.

A nearby mound in Ross's Landing, one of many such earthworks from the Gulf north to Cahokia, Illinois, was evidence that this land had been occupied by Native Americans for centuries and was not empty and free for the taking as many arriving Euro-Americans assumed.

John Melish, the Scottish cartographer and travel-writer, was unimpressed by the mounds. They weren't that high at sixty feet though he admitted they were very wide. He thought they'd been made for relatively recent defense purposes.[11]. Archeaologists would later realize that the mounds were part of an extensive and continuous culture from prehistoric hunter-gatherers dating from 35,000 BCE. The earthworks had been ceremonial centers, and cemeteries with significant cosmological meaning for the many tribes who had lived there successively—the Chicksaws, Choctaws, Creeks, Cherokees.

Ahead of the Honfleurs on their journey were the Blue Ridge Range, with some peaks of more than six thousand feet. The mountains had long been considered an insurmountable barrier to movement east — that is, until the need to get cotton from Alabama, Georgia and Tennesse to Atlantic ports justified digging a tunnel through a small mountain near Ross's Landing. Irish immigrants were used to dig the 1,447 feet-long tunnel because slaves were considered too valuable for owners to risk using for such a dangerous project.

Hectorina recalled that when she was eleven she and her family had travelled over difficult mountain ridges in Pennsylvania, going west then. It was ironic that now she was faced with going east across the mountains of Tennessee and Georgia, a continuation of the same mountain chain.

Since the tunnel under a notch in the Blue Ridge chain wouldn't be finished until May, a month after the Honfleurs wanted to travel, a wagon or stage coach would have taken them over the incline to a train waiting on the other side. She was glad she didn't have to go into that dark hole of a tunnel.

She climbed aboard the train with Juan pushing her up the tall steps. The train moved from thrity to sixty miles an hour, compared to the top speed of a stage coach of five miles an hour. It would take about eight hours to traverse the 387 miles of track to Savannah. They were so tired the motion of the train, gentle as compared with the stage coach, rocked them to sleep immediately in spite of the noise and sooty air blowing throuogh the open windows.

They awoke somewhat rested and watched the monotonous scenery moving by. The fields were freshly plowed as far as the eye could see in every direction,  ready to be planted with cotton seed, not yet the land of white gold it would become in late summer when the fluffy white bolls would be revealed.

No one in the 1700s thought that cotton would grow so far north. But the fear of being outnumbered and slaughtered by blacks as had happened in St. Domingue in 1791 made cotton planters want to abandon the Caribbean islands altogether and try growing cotton in the American South. John Melish tallied up the populations of the southern states using a census and was relieved to see the ratio of whites to blacks was two to one.[12] But that was in 1818. In 1850, blacks outnumbered whites. Indeed, Hectorina saw only enslaved blacks out the train window. Although some were planting cotton in the fields, others were laying train tracks. Owners found they made more money renting out slaves than using them in the fields. Ironically the Union Army under General Sherman, with the help, perhaps, of many of these same slaves she saw out the window, would rip up the tracks as they marched east to victory just fourteen years later in the Civil War.

From a distance as Hectorina looked out the window, it seemed perfectly natural to regard the enslaved as beasts of burden, not people with deep emotions like her own. Melish held that opinion too before he had an experience that affected him to the core of his being. He was near Wheeling, Virginia (now West Virginia) when a man in a skiff drew close to the shore with "four negro children, the oldest about fourteen, the youngest about four years of age. Finding he could dispose of the [negro] man by the way to advantage, he had sold him. The night after, the woman . . . had run away . . . The three youngest had not reflection enough to feel their loss; they jumped out of the boat, and played about upon the sand. But the eldest sat in the boat, the emblem of heart-rending grief and despair!—I did not know that in the whole course of my life I ever had my feelings so severely tried. I hid my face with my hands, that those accustomed to such scenes might not perceive my weakness."[13] It is doubtful Hectorina ever had such an experience where she saw enslaved Africans with emotions like hers.

In Savannah, the Honfleurs descended the train steps into the soggy and sultry April air. They had been travelling since the end of March and were just a short steamboat ride from St. Augustine. They looked forward to a breeze over the water and a comfortable bed in the recently renovated hotel.

They debarked at the St. Johns River docks and took a carriage to their hotel. Hectorina, not having been to Europe, must have been charmed by the ancient town founded by the Spanish in 1565—its narrow streets and its houses with loggias and balconies, made from tabby (a mixture of lime, sand and shells). Arriving at the hotel, they signed in: "Visitors at the Magnolia House, April 4 [1850] Honfleur, Lady and servt. Nashville."[14] Up in their room, the view overlooking the river and ocean was entrancing. The next day they walked the block or two to Ann's house on Avilés Street, at the corner of

Hospital Street, near the plaza and the slave market. Everyone knew who she was and where her house was; it was a small town and she had lived there for three decades.

Juan left the two women to visit while he worked on an advertisement to place in the local newspaper for art lessons in St. Augustine. Ann told Hectorina about her brother, John Fraser, and how he had drowned when his clipper ship had run aground entering the St. Johns River on a return trip from Africa in 1813, at forty-four years of age. John chose four fellow slave traders and close friends, one of them also married to an African woman, to distribute his property as executors, spread as it was over three continents. When one executor travelled to Inverness in 1817 to give Ann her legacy and that of her deceased brother, Archibald, totaling $8,800, she was outraged to learn that John had left the remainder of his estate of $300,000 ($4,700,000 today) to his five mulatto children by his African wife, Phenda.[15]

Within a year, Ann, her husband William and daughter, Margaret, had come to Florida to challenge the will. William died a few years after their arrival. Nevertheless, Ann continued to work with the lawyers they'd hired. Her lawyers argued that not John but his executors had written the will and that, in any case, Africans could not inherit money. What John had written of Phenda in his will incensed Ann: "[Phenda] is a very sensible woman, and of a clear mind, and as such would not meet with contempt in a country where little attention is paid to colour."[16]

John owned several holding pens in Africa for slaves, as well as storehouses, known as factories, one of which his "woman Phenda" managed. He also owned three very large slave plantations on Amelia Island, Florida—two for rice, corn and indigo for dyeing cloth, totaling five hundred acres, and one for cotton of three thousand acres— as well as properties in South Carolina and England. He had shifted his slaves from Charleston, South Carolina, to newly acquired land in the Spanish colony of East Florida after slave importation had been outlawed in the U. S. in 1808.

A few years after Ann and William's arrival, when they still had not resolved their dispute with the will, Florida was ceded by Spain to the U. S., becoming a territory in 1821 and then in 1845 a state in the Union, making the probate of Fraser's estate even more complex. After thirty years of legal wrangling, Ann won a third of the estate. Phenda and all but one of their five mulatto children had died. The remainder went to the lawyers and executors.[17]

Sometime in their four-day visit, Ann might have taken Hectorina on a carriage ride to see John's former plantations, which by then had mostly been sold or leased. If so, Hectorina perhaps was surprised to see the destruction of crops and buildings on his former land. Ann explained that the Seminoles, having been ordered by the federal government to cede their land had been joined by escaped slaves, a coalition known as the Black Seminoles. They had marauded plantations of the hated owners and had set fire to John's property in the confusingly named Patriots War of 1812. The suppression of the insurrection was cast by the American military as defending white "patriots." In truth, the government was trying to evict Seminoles from their land. No place in the world was as perfect for growing cotton and the seizing of it would be enormously profitable for the American government.

The U.S. troops failed, however, and the territory was returned to Spain in 1814. Almost continuous guerilla warfare continued for the next few years until in 1816 U.S. troops invaded again, wresting East Florida from Spain, in what was known as the First Seminole War (1816-18). In 1830, the U. S. government passed the Indian Removal Act and started to forcibly seize the land and marched the indigenous people out of Florida in the Second Seminole War.

The Seminole journey to Oklahoma, like the Cherokee journey, was called the Trail of Tears. In 1844, Ann's daughter, Margaret, married one of the soldiers whom she would have met during the Second Seminole War.

During Ann's decades-long residence in Florida, she became friendly with one of the executors of her brother's estate, Thomas Napier. He may have encouraged her to go into the slave trade herself for she is recorded as the owner of a forty-ton ship, the *William Seabrook*, in manifests of slave ships sailing into the Port of Savannah in 1844.[18] Though the ports from which the ships sailed are not specified in these manifests, they would have sailed from American coastal cities, such as Baltimore, Charleston, Jacksonville, Mobile, New Orleans and St. Augustine because importing slaves from Africa had been outlawed in 1808. It may seem unusual that Ann was involved in the slave trade, but in fact, women's direct involvement in slave trading was common, especially in the nineteenth century, according to historian Stephanie Jones-Rogers.[19]

Hectorina learned that most of the value of John's estate, like that of the majority of planters, was not so much in land and crops, but in the enslaved. Three hundred seventy-five of John's were considered valuable "Prime Africans," as judged by dealers who had observed them working.[20] From similar observations, Ann also had become skilled at estimating an enslaved person's financial worth, considering primarily his health, strength and skills or, in the case of a woman, her childbearing potential and domestic skills.

Ann had inherited eight house slaves,[21] whom she treated disdainfully. To Hectorina slavery was a familiar fact of lfe. It was only the small scale of slavery in Illinois compared to that of the area around St. Augustine and the rest of the Deep South that surprised her. Three hundred eighty-eight-thousand slaves were imported from Africa while the population had grown within America to three million two hundred thousand.

On another visit with Ann a few days later, Hectorina found her very ill. She was shaking and, in her delirium, pushing away her slaves and even Hectorina when they tried to help. She had "the fever," her slaves told Hectorina. The next day, April 9, 1850, Ann was dead, and three days later, on April 12, so was Hectorina, at forty-three.[22] Both had been bitten by mosquitos infected with the yellow fever virus.

According to John Duffy in *Yellow Fever in the Continental US during the Nineteenth Century*, "The attacks [of yellow fever] increased in intensity and severity until the 1850's, when a series of devastating epidemics struck every coastal city from Norfolk, Va., to Brownsville, Texas. These years mark the peak of yellow fever in the United States."[23]

After Hectorina's death, Juan moved on to Athens, Georgia, where he married Annie Whitaker, nineteen, on October 12, 1850. [24] In the December 1850 Alabama census Juan was living at age forty-six with an Anice (or Annie) Honfleur, age nineteen. Another in the household is E. H. Whitaker, female old enough to be her mother.[25]

Meanwhile, Ann's daughter, Margaret, buried her mother next to her father in the Huguenot Cemetery, outside the limits of the Catholic city of St. Augustine. It is ironic that Thomas Napier, who had helped Ann in the business of slave trading, described her as "a woman of truth, Christian humility and of pure piety."[26]

Hectorina's obituary written in a similar vein, reads, "As she lived so she died—a humble Christian." She may have been responsible for persuading Ann to leave a $5,000 bequest to the Presbyterian Missionary Society in Philadelphia in her will, since Ann was not known to have any ties to that city, and the PMS was a charity that Hectorina's oldest sister, Mary, had given to.[27] It seems likely that it was Margaret who buried Hectorina as well in the Huguenot Cemetery outside the city limits, for there is a marker there.[28] Perhaps one or both of Hectorina's sons later moved her remains to Shawneetown. In any case, there is a headstone for her not only in St. Augustine, but also in Shawneetown's Westwood Cemetery, near those of her sisters, Mary, Jane and Rachel Magdalene, and her brother, Seignelay.

The Ridgway-Grant plot in Westwood Cemetery, dominated by the obelisk of Mary Grant and John Ridgway, stood sentinel over many floods of the Ohio River, sometimes reaching the second story of the enormous riverfront Greek Revival bank which belonged to Tom Ridgway, Mary and John Ridgway's son, until in 1937 a large flood destroyed Old Shawneetown. Any buildings that could be salvaged were moved inland.

# CONCLUSION

AFTER HECTORINA'S DEATH IN 1850, only one of John and Jean Grant's children, also named John, may have been alive. A merchant like his father, John had settled with his wife and children in northern Indiana. What little is known of him is gleaned from Mary's and Alexander's letters. Census records are spotty for this area near Lake Michigan.

The American Grant grandchildren continued to make their homes in the Midwest, for the most part, and were leading citizens, judges, hotel owners, politicians, bankers and merchants, or married them, enjoying comfortable lives. One grandson, Mary and John Ridgway's son, served a term as Illinois State Treasurer. Hectorina's two boys by two fathers were successful carpenters and builders.

The Grant relatives in Scotland did not fare so well. With few opportunities to better themselves, they struggled with poverty and famine in the 1840s —along with the Irish. Saddened by the state of his flock a minister in the district where the Grant family lived remarked on their pride and hardiness in 1837: "Poverty having tended greatly to crush the social feelings of the people, they enjoy in a very limited degree the pleasures or advantages of society yet they are in general not dissatisfied with their condition . . . The few that remain of the old race are greatly reduced in circumstances. . . The poor in this parish do not apply for relief, until compelled by necessity—in any other case they regard it as degradation."[1]

John's brother, William, who had helped him with flax culture, died of unknown causes in middle age, according to Hectorina's 1834 letter, but four of John's siblings remained in the Highlands after 1850. Two sisters, Barbara and Anne, made their homes on the Fairburn estate within a mile or so of the cottage where they had grown up. For the Grant children to be permitted to live on Fairburn there would have been a close bond of some kind between the Mackenzie chief and their father, Alexander Grant, perhaps through his first wife, Christian Mackenzie. Barbara married a ploughman, a day laborer, and lived as a squatter somewhere near Coul House (a Mackenzie hunting lodge on Fairburn), according to a letter sent to her at that address. Anne married a farmer who immigrated to Wisconsin expecting his wife and two daughters to join him. They never did. Perhaps Anne felt responsible for her deaf brother Alexander. Anne, a shopkeeper, according to the census, lived in a cottage named Clachuile, also on Fairburn, which she operated as an inn. In photographs of Clachuile today, it is about fifteen by thirty feet, very like her father's. After Anne's death in 1855, her daughters continued to run the inn. Sister Catherine taught spinning in SSPCK schools until they were no longer needed in an age of factory-made cloth. What she did to support herself after that isn't known. She and Alexander both died at Clachuile in 1860, according to their death certificates, no doubt cared for in their last years by Anne's daughters.

Aunt Catherine gave the treasured letters from America to a daughter of Anne. Four generations later a descendant of that daughter found them in 2007 while clearing out her Canadian parents' home. She had never heard any mention of them though they were labelled "Grant Letters Important." I am grateful that her interest in the letters led her to look for our family tree on the internet and that she shared them with me before giving them to the Highland Archive Centre in Inverness. I would never have found the letters then, as there are hundreds of John Grants and Jean Frasers indexed there. Indeed letters of several John Grants were sent me, which were clearly not those of my John Grant.

◆━━━━◆━━━━◆

By 1850, the cotton industry, which had been thriving in Glasgow when John was there in 1807, was in decline. Worker strikes, restrictions on child labor and shifting of workers to the coal and iron industries contributed to the cotton mills' demise.

The British Empire, on the other hand, was at the apex of its ascendancy over the cotton industry in 1850. Mills in Manchester, unlike those in Scotland, were thriving, because child labor was still permitted. The prospect of the loss of child labor, however, was minor compared to the industry's dependence on slave labor in the American South. British capitalists watched the growing Abolition movement in America with increasing apprehension. With the first shots at Fort Sumter in 1861, their fears were realized. Panic gripped financial markets from Bombay to Hong Kong as American exports of raw cotton to Britain dwindled to a halt. Owners closed their mills and laid off workers, as the British government desperately and unsuccessfully searched for another source of free or inexpensive and compliant labor, preferably among people of color.

After all the suffering created over three centuries by British capitalists' efforts to produce and export inexpensive cotton around the world, its cotton empire lasted only eighty years, from 1780–1860.

The good influence of the Grant family, however, continued for eighty years after their deaths. "It may be said of this family," wrote John M. Palmer in *Bench and Bar in Illinois* published in 1899, "that in the early days of Shawneetown and vicinity it had precedence in point of education, refinement and deep piety, and as such it became a special blessing to the community; its elevating influence is still notice-able there. Alexander Fraser Grant, [the son], was one of a number of men who studied law in the office of Hon. Henry Eddy and afterward was appointed judge of the circuit court. . .During his somewhat pro-tracted illness he was tenderly watched and cared for, in addition to the loving ministrations of his sister, by Messrs. Lincoln, Eddy, Browne and other warm personal friends. . .His moral and intellectual excel-lencies and pleasing manners won him universal respect and esteem."

It is encouraging to note that lives well lived can outlast empires.

# ACKNOWLEDGMENTS

I am indebted to Alison Hicks' early help and that of her Greater Philadelphia Wordshop Studio. Novelist Janet Benton read an early version of the book and gave me many valuable suggestions about how to proceed. Varsana Tikovsky read the book near its completion combing it for errors. Any errors remaining are mine.

This book couldn't have been written without the generosity of Iona Loosen who gave me photocopies and transcriptions of the Grant letters to Scotland, before giving them to the Highland Centre Archive. I am grateful to Sarah Bent at Walnford for transcriptions and photocopies of the Ridgway letters to Sarah Waln from Illinois.

Peter Mennie at the Highland Archive Center provided me with letters from the Alexander Fraser file written by John Grant. I wish also to thank the helpful librarians at the Historical Society of Pennsylvania, and at White County Illinois Library and Courthouse.

Catherine Durant Voorhees, encouraged me to complete this story and was a helpful companion during this project providing much valued research.

I wish to give special thanks to my son, Richard, who shared his knowledge of genealogy and technical expertise. His posting of our family tree on ancestry.com linked us to the Grant letters to Scotland from Philadelphia and Illinois.

Without the ongoing  scanning of the contents of libraries, newspapers, journals, parish records and the like, which began in 1994, and  the invention  of search engines like Google that connect scanned books through links and tags to one another, I was able to travel in my home to libraries in distant countries.

And finally, no words can express my love and gratitude to my husband— for his tolerance of my total emersion and mental absence while writing, for his reading of many drafts of this book, and for his thoughtful suggestions.

# NOTES

1.    HCA Highland Archive Centre, Bught Road Inverness IV3 555

2.    Monmouth County Park Systems Archives Historic Walnford, 62 Walnford Road Allentown NJ 08501

3.    Reference Guide of University of Strathclyde  was used  for citing Scottish sources.
      https://www.strath.ac.uk/media/1newwebsite/centres/centreforlife-longlearning/documents/Referencing_Guide.pdf

## Introduction

1.    Sven Beckert, *Empire of Cotton: A Global History* (New York: Vintage Books, 2015), 452, note 4.

2.    Beckert, 441.

## Chapter One

1.    W.H.K. Turner, "Flax cultivation in Scotland: An Historical Geography," *Transactions of the Institute of British Geographers*, no. 55 (1972): 127-143, https://www.jstor.org/stable/621726?seq=1#metadata_info_tab_contents.

2.    Sir John Sinclair, ed., *The Statistical Account of Scotland, Urray, Ross and Cromarty*, Vol. 7 Edinburgh: William Creech, 1793), 248, 252.

The Statistical Accounts online: http://stataccscot.edina.ac.uk/link/osa-vol7-p248-parish-ross_and_cromarty-urray.

3.  Annette Carruthers, ed., *The Scottish Home* (Edinburgh: National Museum of Scotland, 1996), 37–58.

4.  Margaret Connell Szasz, *Scottish Highlanders and Native Americans: Indigenous Education in the Eighteenth-Century Atlantic World* (Norman: University of Oklahoma Press, 2007), 82.

5.  *Ibid.*, 82.

6.  A. S. Cowper, ed., *SSPCK Schoolmasters 1709–1872*, (Edinburgh: Scottish Record Society, 1997), 34.

7.  Szasz, 82-87.

8.  Alexander Grant, Session Clerk, 22 January 1773-January 1775, CH2/1136/145-171, Minutes of Rosskeen Session, 145–49, obtained through https://www.oldscottish.com/homeback.html Look-up Report, retrieved 7 January 2019.

9.  Szasz, 13.

10. James Miller, *Inverness* (Edinburgh: Birlinn, 2004), 137-147.

11. *Ibid.*, 147.

12. *Ibid.*, 144.

13. Sinclair, vol 9, 635.

14. Baptisms, *Old Parish Registers*, 061/10 126  03/01/1769, GRANT, John, 126. http://www.scotlandspeople

15. John Grant to Alexander Grant and Alexander Fraser, 12 July 1811, HCA/D1108, Grants in U.S.A.

16. Sinclair, Vol. 9, 617.

17. Sinclair, Vol. 7, 252.

18. Douglas. J. Hamilton, *Scotland, The Caribbean and the Atlantic World, 1750–1820* (Manchester: Manchester University Press, 2005), 1.

19. David Alston, Slaves & Highlanders, James Baillie Fraser, accessed March 2019, http://www.spanglefish.com/slavesandhighlanders/index.asp?pageid=223587

20. David Alston, Slaves & Highlanders, William Fraser of Culbokie, accessed March 2019. http://www.spanglefish.com/slavesandhighlanders/index.asp?pageid=226600

21. David Alston Slaves & Highlanders, Henry Dalton, accessed March 2019. http://www.spanglefish.com/SlavesandHighlanders/index.asp?pageid=164652

22. Baptisms, *Old Parish Registers*, 098/60, 16 July 1802, GRANT, Mary Fraser, 222, http://www.scotlandspeople/

23. Mary Grant Ridgway to Catherine Grant, 22 January 1836, with enclosed obituary of Alexander Grant, HCA/D1108, Grants in U.S.A.

24. Baptisms, *Old Parish Registers*, 644/1 200, 20 January 1807, GRANT, Hectorina Kennedy, 347, http://www.scotlandspeople/

25. Anthony Cooke, *The Rise and Fall of the Scottish Cotton Industry, 1778-1914: The Secret Spring* (Manchester: Manchester University Press, 2010), 4.

26. *Ibid.*, 12.

27. *Ibid.*, 51.

28. Robert Southhey, *Journal of a Tour in Scotland, 1819*, "Utopia," Quoted in Jennings, Humphrey, *Pandaemonium 1660–1886: The Coming of the Machine As Seen By Contemporary Observers*, Mary Lou Jennings and Charles Madge, eds., (New York: The Free Press, 1985), 156-158.

29. Quoted in Cooke, 55.

30. John Grant to Alexander Grant and Alexander Fraser, 24 February 1812, HCA/D1108, Grants in U.S.A.

**Chapter Two**

1. GRANT, John, Alien report, 1812 July 24, No 109.United States Special District Court of Pennsylvania City, Philadelphia. Private Collection.

2.  John Malcolm Bulloch, *Territorial Soldiering in the Northeast of Scotland, 1759–1814* (Aberdeen: Aberdeen University, 1914), 34.

3.  *Bench and Bar in Illinois,* New London County, Connecticut, 1899. (New York: publisher not transcribed) https://.loc.gov/item209696888/. vol. 2, 854.

4.  GRANT, John, Petition to become a citizen of United States, 1817 July 25 No 109 United States Special District Court of Pennsylvnaia City, Philadelphia. Private Collection.

5.  John Grant to Alexander Grant and Alexander Fraser, 24 February 1812, HCA/D1108, Grants in U.S.A.

6.  John Grant to Alexander Grant and Alexander Fraser, 8 July 1819, HCA./D1108, Grants in the U.S.A.

7.  Mary Grant to Catherine Grant, care of Alexander Fraser, 3 June 1811, HCA/D1108, Grants in U. S.A.

8.  Bruce Mouser, ed., *A Slaving Voyage to Africa and Jamaica* (Bloomington: Indiana University Press, 2002), 7.

9.  *Ibid.,* footnote, 57.

10. "Liverpool and the Atlantic Slave Trade," Maritime Archives Temporary Exhibit, Merseyside Maritime Museum, National Museums Liverpool, accessed 19 March 2019, http://www.liverpoolmuseums.org.uk/maritime/archive/info-sheet.aspx?sheetId=3

11. John Grant to Alexander Grant and Alexander Fraser, Inverness, 27 September 1818, HCA/D1108, Grants in U.S.A.

12. John Grant to Alexander Grant & Alexander Fraser, Inverness, 12 July 1811, HCA/D1108, Grants in U.S.A.

13. John Grant to Alexander Grant and Alexander Fraser, Inverness, 8 July 1819, HCA/D1108, Grants in U.S.A.

14. Donald Sage, *Memorabilia Domestica: Or, Parish Life in the North of Scotland* (Edinburgh: reprint University of California Libraries, 1899), 42–47.

15. Testamentary Records, Scotland, February 9, 1801. FRASER, John, Inverness Commissary Court CC11/1/6, accessed 7 June 7 2015, https://www.scotlandspeople.gov.uk/view-image/nrs_wills_testaments/297677?image=1

16. Marriages, *Old Parish Registers*, GRANT & FRASER 1/09/1801 098/80 Inverness, 211.

17. Sage, 45.

18. *Ibid.*, 42–47

19. Sinclair, ed., .vol 9, 617.

20. *An Account of the Funds, Expenditures, and General Management of the Affairs of the Scottish Society of Propagation of Christian Knowledge Contained in a Report, Drawn up by a Commission of their Number, Appointed for that Purpose* (Edinburgh: SSPCK, 1796).

21. Baptisms, Old Parish Register, 098/60 16 July 1802, GRANT, Mary. Fraser, 222, http://www.scotlands peoople

22. Alexander Fraser (1746-1818) was a SSPCK Schoolmaster at Raining's Society School in Inverness. Because Alexander supported his brother's grocery business while teaching, he was told "to choose between teaching and trading. He resigned." Cowper, 31. All letters to Alexander Grant include Alexander Fraser's name, HCA/D1108, Grants in U.S.A.

23. *Missionary Magazine*, Vol. 5, 1899 (Edinburgh: J. Pillans & Sons, 1900), 401.

24. "Foulah Mission," *Evangelical Magazine*, Vol. 5, (November 1797).

25. *Missionary Magazine*, 128.

26. David Alston, Slaves & Highlanders "Alexander Fraser of Kirkhill," http://www.spanglefish.com/SlavesandHighlanders/index.asp?pageid=225143127. Accessed 19 March 2019.

27. John Calvin, *Commentaries on Isaiah 49–66* (Altenmuster,Germany:Jazzybee Verlag, 2012) Kindle.

28. Billy G. Smith, *Ship of Death: A Voyage That Changed the Atlantic World* (New Haven: Yale University Press, 2013).

29. Francois Barbe-Marbois, *Histoire de la Louisiane*, quoted in Francois Furstenberg, *When the United States Spoke French: Five Refugees Who Shaped a Nation* (New York: Penguin 2014), 399-401.

30. Immigrant Ships Transcriber's Guild: Ship *Wm Little John*, Vol. 9, accessed 11 December 2018, https://www.immigrantships.net/v9/1800v9/wmlittlejohn18000428.html

31. Mouser, 18–19.

32. Mouser, 26.

33. John Grant to Alexander Grant and Alexander Fraser, 27 September 1818, HCA/D1108, Grants in U.S.A.

34. Laura Ricketson Doherty, *Annie Ricketson's Journal* (Berwyn, Maryland: Heritage Books, 2010), 60.

35. Frederick M. Miller, *Philadelphia Immigrant City*, Historical Society of Pennsylvania exhibit on length of voyage up Delaware.

36. Wayne Franklin, *The Life of James Fenimore Cooper* (New Haven: Yale University Press, 2007), 38, 97-98.

37. News of British firing on American frigate, shouted to Grant's ship, was compiled from headlines in *Carlisle Gazette*, 3 July, 1807; *Herald Office Norfolk*, 23 June, 1807.

## Chapter Three

1. George Wilson, *Stephen Girard: The Life and Times of America's First Tycoon* (Conshohocken, Pennsylvaia: Combined Books, 1995), 200.

2. Henry Kyriakodis, *Philadelphia's Lost Waterfront* (Charleston, SC: The History Press, 2011), 10.

3. Abraham Ritter, *Philadelphia and her Merchantst*, (Philadelphia: Ritter, 1860), 19-23.

4. Wilson, 334.

5. John Woolf Jordan, *Colonial Families of Philadelphia*, (Phildelphia, Pennsylannia: Lewis Publishing Company, 1911), 890.

6. Cope's estate was $1,474,000. http://web.tri-colib.brynmawr.edu/speccoll/dictionary/index.php/COPE,_Thomas_P._(Thomas_Pim),_1768-1854

7. Kyriakodis, 89.

8. John Melish, *Melish's Travels*, Vol. 19 (Carlisle, Massachusetts: Applewood Books Reprints, 1818), 116.

9. Norfolk Herald, 29 June, 1807 Virginia https://www.genealogybank.com/doc/newspapers/image/v2%3A-109505F75A0331E8%40GB3NEWS-1096BFCA6B09A B70%402381232-1096BFCB7B9A6470%402-1096BF-CC9A57E580%40From%2Bthe%2BNorfolk%2BHer-ald?h=1&fname=&mname=&lname=&kwinc=The%20whole%20 of%20the%20country%20is%20ripe%20for%20revenge%20 frigate&kwexc=&rgfromDate=06/1807&rgtoDate=1807&form-Date=&formDateFlex=exact&dateType=range&processing-time=&addedFrom=&addedTo=&sid=axxdzsarpmkmgqoxjew-cyrkrentkzqzx_wma-gateway009_1590429991240

10. Thomas Cope, *Philadelphia Merchant, Diary of Thomas P. Cope, 1800–1851*, Eliza Cope Harrison, ed., (South Bend, IN: Gateway, 1978), 216.

11. James Robinson, *Philadelphia Directory, 1807, containing the Names, Trades and Residence of the Inhabitants of the City, Southwark, and the Northern Liberties*, (Philadelphia: Philadelphia Publishers).

12. Ritter, 23.

13. Emanuel Walker, born 16 July 1730, Port Glasgow, son of Emanuel Walker and Euphemia Porterfield.

14. They used Ross's, Walnut Street and Cooper's wharves.

15. *Porcupine Gazette*, Vol. I, Issue 39, 153. Earliest record of partnership is April 18, 1797. https://www.genealogy-bank.com/doc/newspapers/image/v2%3A10CEBB6D-02C5C720%40GB3NEWS-10E58270F05E5300%40237 8096-10E582718C1959E0%403-10E5827347C7E1E0% 40Advertisement?lname=walker&dateType=range&form-

DateFlex=exact&rgtoDate=1798&rgfromDate=1796

16. John Grant to Alexander Grant and Alexander Fraser, 12 July 1811. HCA/D1108, Grants in U.S.A.

17. Robinson, *Philadelphia Directory*, 1807.

18. Hannah Brittenham Summers, born 1783, Ancestry.com, accessed http://www.ancestry.com/search/?name=Hannah+brittenham. Summers&birth=1783

19. *Finlay's American Naval and Commercial Register*, Vol. 1, Issue 222, (Philadelphia: S. Finlay) 2.

20. Domenic Vitiello, with George E. Thomas, *The Philadelphia Stock Exchange and the City It Made* (Philadelphia: University of Pennsylvania Press, 2010), xii–50.

21. William Woys Weaver, *35 Receipts from The Larder Invaded* (Philadelphia: Library Company of Philadelphia, Historical Society of Pennsylvania, 1986), 40–42.

22. Mary Anne Hines, Gordon Marshall and William Woys Weaver, *The Larder Invaded: Reflections on Three Centuries of Philadelphia Food and Drink* (Philadelphia: Library Company of Philadelphia, Historical Society of Pennsylvania, 1987), 27.

23. Hines, 25.

24. William Woys Weaver, *A Quaker Woman's Cookbook* (Mechanicsburg, PA: Stackpole Books, 2004), 10.

25. Cope, 212–13.

26. Brian Lavery, ed., *Shipboard Life and Organisation, 1731–1815* (Brookfield, VT: Ashgate Publishing, 1998), 239–417.

## Chapter Four

1. Douglas A. Irwin, "The Welfare Cost of Autarky: Evidence from the Jeffersonian Trade Embargo, 1807–1809, *Review of International Economics* Vol. 13, No. 4, 2005, 631–45.

2. Leah Blackman, *Little Egg Harbor Township* (Trenton, NJ: Trenton Printing Co., 1963), 279–80.

3. John Grant to Alexander Fraser, 10 June 1809, HCA/D122/2/4.

4. Cope, 230.

5. *Poulson's American Daily Advertiser* (Philadelphia, Pennsylvania), December 2, 1808 https://www.genealogybank.com/doc/newspapers/image/v2%3A10380B4ABA623678%40GB-3NEWS-1047482EAA73BDFC%402381754-1047482EB93F29BA%400-1047482F909406D2%40Advertisement?h=24&fname=&mname=&lname=Grant&rgfromDate=1808&rgtoDate=1808&formDate=&formDateFlex=exact&dateType=range&kwinc=Front%20street&kwexc=&page=1&sid=gdbuejscnjtvmikwuuwnkztlrcsny-hsf_wma-gateway003_1590432998612https://www.genealogybank.com/doc/newspapers/image/v2%3A10380B4ABA623678%40GB-3NEWS-10474D0E2BA2243A%402382459-10474D0E3850F5BD%400-10474D0EFB20AD64%40Advertisement?h=36&fname=&mname=&lname=Grant&kwinc=Front%20street%20&kwexc=&rgfromDate=1808&rgtoDate=1812&formDate=&formDateFlex=exact&dateType=range&processingtime=&addedFrom=&addedTo=&page=2&sid=eobfurmwakbxongwaidoresfihqqafdn_wma-gateway016_1590433771046

6. Wilson, 94–95.

7. Ritter, 163–64.

8. Amy Henderson, *Furnishing the Republican Court* (Wilmington, DE: Dissertation, University of Delaware, 2005), 182.

9. *Poulson's American Daily Advertiser*, October 31, 1808. https://www.genealogybank.com/doc/newspapers/image/v2%3A10380B4ABA623678%40GB3NEWS-1047482EAA73BDFC%402381754-1047482EB93F29BA%400-1047482F909406D2%40Advertisement?h=24&fname=&mname=&lname=Grant&rgfromDate=1808&rgtoDate=1808&formDate=&formDateFlex=exact&dateType=range&kwinc=Front%20street&kwexc=&page=1&sid=gdbuejscnjtvmikwuuwnkztlrcsny-hsf_wma-gateway003_1590432998612

10. John Grant to Alexander Fraser, 10 June 1809, HCA/D122/2/4.

11. *Poulson's American Daily Advertiser*, January 1, 1813, Vol. XIII, Issue 11267, 4.

12. Billy G. Smith, *The Lower Sort: Philadelphia's Laboring People, 1750–1800* (Ithaca, NY: Cornell University, 1990), 163.

13. *Ibid.*, 28.

14. Robinson, *Philadelphia Directory*,

15. Administration of Estate of John Grant, 21 August 1820 (Carmi: White County Clerk of Circuit Court).

16. Mary Grant to Catherine Grant, 3 June, 1811, HCA/D1108, Grants in U.S.A.

17. John Grant to Alexander Grant and Alexander Fraser, 12 July 1811, HCA/D1108, Grants in U.S.A.

18. Roy Goodman and David Orr, "Northern Liberties, Workshop of the World, "Sprague's Philadelphia Carpet Manufactory," https://www.workshopoftheworld.com/northern_liberties/northern_liberties.html

19. https://libwww.freelibrary.org/digital/item/43942

20. http://www.bluebookofpianos.com/chronicals.html

21. Administration of Estate of John Grant, 21 August 1820 (Carmi: White County Clerk of Circuit Court).

22. Alexander Grant to Catherine Grant, 18 March 1826, HCA/D1108, Grants in  U.S.A.

23. Administration of Estate of John Grant, 21 August 1820, (Carmi: White County Clerk of Circuit Court).

24. Szasz, 111.

25. *Philadelphia Repository and Weekly Register*, Philadelphia, PA, March 14, 1801, Vol. 1, Issue 18, 7.

26. Mary Grant to Catherine Grant, 3 June 1811, HCA/D1108, Grants in U.S.A.

27. https://www.genealogybank.com/doc/census/image/
    v2%3A16DABE9A383D710A%40GB3CENSUS-16DABC-
    DA43025AF0%402382149-16EBAB4305650C92%40?per-
    son=p_10417397036

28. Administration of John Grant Estate, 21 August 1820 (Carmi:
    White County Clerk of Circuit Court).

29. John Grant to Alexander Grant and Alexander Fraser, 12 July 1811,
    HCA/D1108, Grants in U.S.A.

30. John Grant to Alexander Fraser, 10 June 1809,
    HCA/D/122/2/4.

31. James Hamilton and Co. of Scotland v John Grant 1812,
    (Edinburgh:National Archives of Scotland, CS38/5/130. of
    Scotland) NRS reference RH2/4.

**Chapter Five**

1. Cope, 268.

2. John Grant to Alexander Grant and Alexander Fraser, 24 February
   1812. HCA/D1108, Grants in U.S.A.

3. Cope, 270, 273.

4. Elizabeth Elbourne, *Blood Ground* (Montreal: McGill Queen's
   University Press, 2002), 49.

5. Cope, 298.

6. Richard Hunter, Nadine Sergejeff and Damon Tvaryanas, "Trenton
   Textiles and the Eagle Factory," Trenton Historical Society, http://
   www.trentonhistory.org/Documents/EagleFactory.html

7. *Poulson's American Daily Advertiser*, January 2, 1813, Vol. XLII, Issue
   11267, 4.

8. J. A. Paxton, *Philadelphia Directory*, 1813.

9. Robinson, *Philadelphia Directory*, Robinson,1816, Robinson,1817, J.
   A. Paxton 1818

10. *Boston Recorder*, April 24, 1824, Vol. IX, Issue 17, 3, 67, https://www.genealogybank.com/doc/newspapers/image/ v2%3A109E455E6E63DEA8%40GB3NEWS-13EEE8FBB-38B8E80%402387376-13ED91CCF83407F0%402-13FB8 934048A860C%40Domestic?h=6&fname=&mname=&l-name=&kwinc=New%20York%20Philadelphia%20 imports&kwexc=&rgfro

11. Hector Kennedy married a widow Henrietta Clarke in New York. *New York Daily Advertiser*, May 7, 1817, https://www. genealogybank.com/doc/newspapers/image/v2%3A10D-3492BEC0FE070%40GB3NEWS-10D7F27894E73628%402384 832-10D7F278E33D60A8%401-10D7F27AB9173430%40Matri-mony%2BNotice?h=2&fname=Hector&mname=&lname=Kenne-dy&kwinc

12. Hannah Summers died January 1809, Ancestry.com, _1https:// www.ancestry.com/search/categories/34/?name=Hannah+bRIT-TENHAM_Summers&death=1809_philadelphia-philadel-phia-pennsylvania-usa_15153&death_x=_1-1&spouse=Hector_ kENNEDY

13. Emanuel Walker and Hector Kennedy's partnership dissolved. *Poulson's American Daily Advertiser*, January 4, 1811, Vol. XL, Issue 10658, 1, 3.

14. Kennedy Obituary *Commercial Advertiser*, June 20, 1828, 3, https://www.genealogybank.com/doc/newspapers/image/ v2%3A1044E924036998A0%40GB3NEWS-12FF97B20927 0868%402388894-12FF4A76624F2078%402-1311EFD604B-B3684%40Mortuary%2BNotice?h=1&fname=Hector&m

15. Caleb Ridgway's woolen factory set on fire *American Telegraph*, Brownsville, Pennsylvania, September 6, 1815, Vol. 1, Issue 44, 2, https://www.genealogybank.com/doc/ newspapers/image/v2%3A1080E48162D01818%40GB-3NEWS-10849CA1EB514778%402384211-10849C A23A1E4BC0%401-10849CA353A22F20%40Tren-ton%252C%2BAug.%2B14?h=2&lname=Ridgway&fname=-Caleb&kwinc=woolen&kwexc=&dateType=range&formDate=&-

formDateFlex=&rgfromDate=&rgtoDate=&group=&type=news-paper_articles&sid=vlofaaeheprdicianvvijpbahnjvookp_wma-gate-way001_1591041023793

16. Caleb Ridgway, Quaker Meeting Minutes 4 July 1804 Upper Springfield Monthly Meeting Minutes 1802-1821 New Jersey https://www.ancestry.com/search/collections/2189/?name=-Caleb_Ridgway&f-C000000F=Disownment&residence=1804

17. Cope, 394.

18. Jordan, 887-93.

19. Leah Blackman, *Little Egg Harbor* (Trenton, NJ: Trenton Printing, 1963), 269.

20. Quoted in *Ibid.*, 276–77.

21. Quoted in *Ibid.*, 276.

22. *Ibid.*, 263.

23. Jordan, 891.

24. *Ibid.*, 891.

25. *Ibid.*, 891.

26. Szasz, 3–14.

27. *Philadelphia Gazette*, April 27, 1818, 1. https://www.genealogybank.com/doc/newspapers/image/v2%3A10CEB64FEBA73778%40GB-3NEWS-153C1A837809DEF8%402385183-153B83BADA9A0B18%402

28. *Poulson's American Daily Advertiser*, Vo.XLVII, Issue 12984, 4, https://www.genealogybank.com/doc/newspapers/image/v2%3A10380B4ABA623678%40GB3NEWS-105616D90D7F4AC7%402385255-105616D99110A030%403-105616DB19EA2372%

**Chapter Six**

1. John Grant to Alexander Grant and Alexander Fraser, 19 August 1819, HCA/D1108, Grants in U.S.A.

2.   Morris Birkbeck, *Notes on a Journey in America & Letters from Illinois* (New York: Augustus M. Kelley, 1971).

3.   *Ibid.*, 36.

4.   John Grant to Alexander Grant and Alexander Fraser, 27 September 1818, HCA/D1108, Grants in U.S.A.

5.   One of the Germans was Jeremiah Hartenbower, 1800–1876, bound for four years to John Grant, https://www.findagrave.com/memorial/19924669/jeremiah-hartenbower.

6.   John Grant to Alexander Grant and Alexander Fraser, 27 September, 1818. HCA/D1108. Grants in U.S.A.

7.   Helena Ridgway to Sarah Waln, 28 April, 1829 and 3 May, 1830, Courtesy of the Monmouth Couty Park Systems Archives.

8.   Jordan, 891.

9.   Helena Ridgway to Sarah Waln, April 28, 1829, Courtesy of the Monmouth Couty Park Systems Archives.

10.   Rebecca Rawle Ridgway to Sarah Waln, January 10, 1807, Courtesy of the Monmouth County Park Systems Archives.

11.   Birkbeck, 31.

12.   Cope, 330.

13.   Thomas Lippincott, *Full text of Thomas Lippincott a Pioneer of 1811 and his Diary*, https://archive.org/details/jstor-40187004/page/n4/mode/2up

14.   Richard Rhodes, *John James Audubon* (New York: Knopf, 2004), 49.

15.   Quoted in Rhodes, 49.

16.   Stephen E. Ambrose, *Undaunted Courage* (New York: Simon & Schuster, 1996), 105–107.

17.   Melish, 378–79.

18.   John Grant to Alexander Grant and Alexander Fraser, 19 August, 1819. HCA/D1108, Grants in U.S.A.

19.   Helena Ridgway to Sarah Waln, January 14, 1819, Courtesy of the Monmouth County Park Systems Archives.

20. Lucille Lawler, *Gallatin County* (Crossville, Illinois: Lawler, 1968), 17–18.

21. Bill Nunes, "Salt Licks and Slavery in Illinois," *St. Louis Dispatch*, 17 October 2007. https://www.stltoday.com/suburban-journals/salt-licks-and-slavery-in-illinois/article_c0d755b1-9cde-54dc-943e-8717368120af.html

22. Helena Ridgway to Sarah Waln, January 14, 1819, Courtesy of the Monmouth County Park Systems Archives.

23. John Grant to Alexander Grant and Alexander Fraser, 19 August, 1819, HCA/D1108, Grants in U.S.A.

24. Cowper, 34.

## Chapter Seven

1. Carmi Sesquicentennial Commission, *Sesquicentennial of Carmi*, 11. https://www.bookdepository.com/Carmi-Illinois-1816-1966-Carmi-Sesquicentennial-Commission/9780243080892

2. Solon Justus Buck, Illinois in 1818 (Illinois: IllinoisCentennial Commission 1917) 145-146.

3. White County Historical Society, *History of White County Illinois* (Chicago: Inter-State Publishing, 1883), 535.

4. Buck, 145–46.

5. Helena Ridgway to Sarah Waln, January 14, 1819, Courtesy of the Monmouth County Park Systems Archives.

6. Thomas Bulmer, *Empire in Retreat* (New Haven: Yale University Press, 2018), 21, Quoted from Rockwell, *Indian Affairs*, 88.

7. Helena Ridgway to Sarah Waln, January 14, 1819, Courtesy of the Monmouth County Park Systems Archives.

8. Helena Ridgway to Sarah Waln, January 14, 1819, Courtesy of the Monmouth County Archives.

9. Helena Ridgway to Sarah Waln, January 14, 1819, Courtesy of Monmouth County Park Systems Archives.

10. Helena Ridgway to Sarah Waln, January 14, 1819 Courtesy of

Monmouth County Park Systems Archives.

11.  Helena Ridgway to Sarah Waln, January 14, 1819, Courtesy of Monmouth County Park Systems Archives.

12.  Helena Ridgway to Sarah Waln, 23 June, 1819, Courtesy of Monmouth County Park Systems Archives.

13.  John Grant to Alexander Grant and Alexander Fraser, 19 August, 1819, HCA/D1108, Grants in U.S.A.

14.  Birkbeck, 118.

15.  Helena Ridgway to Sarah Waln, 14 January 1819, Courtesy of Monmouth County Park Systems Archive.

16.  *Illinois Gazette*, Shawneetown, Illinois, August 26, 1820, Issue 43, Column D.

## Chapter Eight

1.  Dr. Thomas Shannon was a neighbor. Mary Grant Ridgway named one of her sons after him: Thomas Shannon Ridgway.

2.  John Grant to Alexander Grant and Alexander Fraser, 19 August 1819. HCA/D1108, Grants in U.S.A.

3.  Carmi Sesquicentennial, 11.

4.  *Ibid.*, 11, 15.

5.  There are no death records for Catherine and Janet. In 1819, their father mentioned them, but they are never mentioned in the letters again.

6.  Henry Eddy Papers 1817–75, https://www.library.illinois.edu/ihx/archon/?p=collections/controlcard&id=597

8.  Probate Records 1772–1970, https://www.ancestry.com/search/collections/9048/

9.  Letters of Administration of John Grant, 21 August, 1820, White County Clerk of Circuit Court.

## Chapter Nine

1. Marriage Record for Mary Grant and John Ridgway, (Carmi: White County Clerk of Circuit Court).

2. Mary Grant Ridgway to Sarah Ridgway Waln, 5 August 1823, Courtesy of Monmouth County Park Systems Archives.

3. Mary Grant Ridgwaya to Sarah Ridgway Waln 4 June 1824, Courtesyf of Monmouth County Park Systems Archives.

4. Helena Ridgway to Sarah Ridgway, 25 May 1824, Courtesy of Monmouth County Park Systems Archives.

## Chapter Ten

1. Lawler, 81

2. James Simeone, *Democracy and Slavery in Frontier Illinois* (Illinois: Northern University Press, 2000), 156.

3. Quoted in Buck, 144.

4. Jon Musgrove, *Handbook of Old Gallatin County and Southeastern Illinois* (Illinois: Illinois history.org,Publishing Co., 2002), 65.

5. Simeone, 111.

6. *Ibid.,* 138.

7. Gerald Leonard, *The Invention of Party Politics, Federalism, Popular Sovereignty and Constitutional Development in Jacksonian Illinois* (Chapel Hill North Carolina: University of North Carolina Press, 2002) 113-15.

8. Alexander Grant to Catherine Grant, 13 August 1835 HCA/ D1108, Grants in U.S.A.

9. Alexander Grant to Catherine Grant, 7 October  1834, HCA/ D1108, Grants in U.S.A.

10. Alexander Grant to Catherine Grant, 20  March 1828, HCA/ D1108, Grants in U.S.A.

11. Alexander Grant to Catherine Grant, 7 October 1834,  HCA/ D1108, Grants in U.S.A.

12. Alexander Grant to Catherine Grant, 18 March, 1826, HCA/ D1108, Grants in U.S.A. D1108, Grants in U.S.A.

13. Alexander Grant to Catherine Grant, 20 March 1828, HCA/ D1108, Grants in U.S.A.

14. Mary Grant Ridgway to Catherine Grant, 13 January 1836, HCA/ D1108, Grants in U.S.A.


## Chapter Eleven

1. Hectorina Dake to Catherine Grant, 13 August 1835, HCA/ D1108, Grants in U.S.A.

2. Thomas Clinton Pears Jr., ed., *New Harmony, An Adventure in Happiness, Papers of Thomas and Sarah Pears,* (Indianapolis: Indiana Historical Society, 1933), 17.

3. *Ibid.,* 3.

4. *Ibid.,* 13.

5. *Ibid.,* 13.

6. *Ibid.,* 13.

7. *Ibid.,* 16.

8. *Ibid.,* 34.

9. *Ibid.,* 25.

10. *Ibid.,* 28.

11. *Ibid.,* 27.

12. *Ibid.,* 40.

13. *Ibid.,* 40.

14. *Ibid.,* 33.

15. *Ibid.,* 61.

16. *Ibid.,* 69, 73, 74.

17. *Ibid.,* 68.

18. *Ibid.,* 68.

19. Alexander Grant to Catherine Grant, 13 August, 1835. HCA/ D1108, Grants in U.S.A.

20. John Grant and Alexander Dake, half-brothers, lived in the same household, throughout their lives. John had a wife and children, one named Hectorina. Alexander was single. Alabama 1870 census https://www.genealogybank.com/doc/census/image/ v2%3A16DABE9A383D71A%40GB3CENSUS-16DABD-3C91D3DF90%402404064-16F19C2CD8479F

21. Delos Hughes, *Historic Alabama Courthouses: A Century of Images and Stories,* (Alabama: New South Books, 2016), 28.

## Chapter Twelve

1. *Times Picayune*, New Orleans, June 19, 1842, 2, https://www. genealogybank.com/doc/newspapers/image/v2%3A122BCE-5B718A166%40GB3NEWS-1224360B83A205F0%40239 4006-1223D6431A9D89A0%401-123D8C568F7EF1FF% 40Advertisement?h=2&fname=&mname=&lname=Honfleur&-rgfromDate=06/1842&rgtoDate=06/1842&formDate=&-formDateFlex=exact&dateType=range&kwexc=&sid=vbmktcyb-kazbyhrxfvofeoekkvxgoeag_s075_1591126226138. Juan had taken a nine-day steamboat trip to Shawneetown after completing his week long drawing class starting on June 27 in New Orleans. Hectorina married Juan Honfleur July 20, 1842, http://genealogytrails.com/ ill/gallatin/groomsg-l.html.

2. From the *Louisville Journal*, An Elopement, June 13, 1838, Gloucester, Massachusets, *Gloucester Telegraph* https:// www.genealogybank.com/doc/newspapers/image/v2%3A-123D88A8D6783EEF%40GB3NEWS-12729B6B0AD7F870% 402392539-12729B6B28B259A8%401-12729B6BC129C290%-40From%2Bthe%2BLouisville%2BJournal%2Ban%2BElopemen-t?fname=j&kwinc=elopement&dateType=range&formDateFlex-=exact&rgtoDate=1839&rgfromDate=1838

3.    *Phoenix Civilian*, Cumberland, Maryland, Vol.XI, Issue 20, August
      3, 1838, 3. *https://www.genealogybank.com/doc/newspapers/image/*
      *v2%3A123FC88033CCD684%40GB3NEWS-126425E359E-*
      *8ACD8%402392605-126425E3C4E23E80%402-1264*
      *25E4DC1AF628%40%255BHonfleur%253B%2BMr.%2BVa-*
      *n%2BBuren%255D?h=1&fname=Honfleur&mname=&lname=Hon-*
      *fleur&kwinc=&kwexc=&lnamer=&rgfromDate=1838&rgto-*
      *Date=1839&formDate=&formDateFlex=exact&dateTy*

4.    *The Commercial Advertiser*, New York, New York , April 8,1839,
      2. https://www.genealogybank.com/explore/newspapers/all/usa/
      new-york/new-york/commercial-advertiser?fname=&mname=&l-
      name=honfleur&rgfromDate=04%2F08%2F1839&rgtoDate=04%

5.    "An Elopement," *The Commercial Advertiser* New York, New
      York, June 8, 1838, 3. https://www.genealogybank.com/doc/
      newspapers/image/v2%3A1044E924036998A0%40GB-
      3NEWS-13044D9C62AEBD08%402392534-13044254710
      E45F8%401-1327933538453AA0%40An%2BElopement?k-
      winc=withal%20an%20ugly%20girl&dateType=range&formDate-
      Flex=exact&rgtoDate=1839&rgfromDate=1838

6.    *The Commercial Advertiser*, New York, New York, 8 April 1839,
      2. https://www.genealogybank.com/explore/newspapers/all/usa/
      new-york/new-york?fname=&mname=&lname=honfleur&rgfrom-
      Date=04/08/1839&rgtoDate=04%25

7.    Cliff, G. Glenn. "KENTUCKY MARRIAGES AND
      OBITUARIES—1787-1860." *Register of Kentucky State Historical
      Society* 36, no. 115 (1938): 158-82. Accessed May 25, 2020.
      www.jstor.org/stable/23371763 https://www.jstor.org/sta-
      ble/23372188?readnow=1&refreqid=excelsior%3Af2cfa96a-
      b70a40f05297dc4e95a2b95d&seq=17#page_scan_tab_contents

8.    Juan taught just one class in Greensboro, Alabama between
      1842-1850 and was by 1850 said to be living in Nashville. See
      Chapter 12, Note 14. https://www.newspapers.com/clip/24030305/
      professor-honfleur/

9. Gad Heuman, James Walvin, eds., *The Slavery Reader*, Daniel L. Schafer, "Family Ties that Bind, Anglo-African slave trader in Africa and Florida, John Fraser and his Descendants," (London: Routledge, 2003), 782.

10. Richard Savage, Jr., *The McMinnville to Chattanooga Stage Road*, Grundy County, Tennessee, (Grundycountyhistorysquarespace.com) https://static1.squarespace.com/static/59c69c542278e-73c826f3226/t/5e0ebb9e389ff14bc0f20dd5/1578023838783/The+McMinnville+to+Chattanooga+Stage+Road.pdf

11. Melish, 347.

12. *Ibid*, 264-266.

13. *Ibid.*, 340-341.

14. *The Ancient City* (St. Augustine Florida: Sylvester Manucy), Vol. 1, 6 April 1850, 3.

15. Schafer, 782.

16. William Robertson and his wife Ann, v. Philip R. Yonge and Zephaniah Kingsley, 1812-1846, Records of Superior Court of East Florida, Box 156 File 59, Exhibit A, 4.

17. Schafer, 786-9

18. Papers of the American Slave Trade: Port of Savannah Slave Manifests 1790-1860 Series D: Records of the U.S. Custom Houses, Reel 3, Frame 0704. http://www.lexisnexis.com/documents/academic/upa_cis/100539_AmSlaveTradeSerDPt1.pdf

19. Stephanie E. Jones-Rogers, *They Were Her Property* (New Haven: Yale University Press, 2019), ix–xx.

20. Schafer, 779.

21. *Ibid.*, 783.

22. Manucy, Vol. 1, 13 April, 1850, 3.

23. John Duffy, "Yellow Fever in the Continental United States During the Nineteenth Century," *Bulletin of the New York Academy of Medicine*, 1968, 694. https://europepmc.org/backend/ptpmcrender.fcgi?accid=PMC1750233&blobtype=pdf.[I

24. Annie Whitaker married Prof J. Honfleur in Raleigh, North Carolina https://www.newspapers.com/image/?clipping_id=5118588&fcfToken=eyJhbGciOiJIUzI1NiIsInR5cCI6IkpXVCJ9.eyJmcmVlLXZpZXctaWQiOjU4MTczNDk5LCJpYXQiOjE1OTEyMDk2NTEsImV4cCI6MTU5MTI5NjA1MX0._jxXPkeaGbeZsL4niWkakL2XhoNaVQeNzowjaoND7Wc

25. E. H. Whitaker living with Annie and Juan. Alabama census 1870 https://www.genealogybank.com/explore/census/all?lname=hONFLEUR&fname=&decade%5B%5D=1850&pq=1&prebuy=no&intver=7D_6M&CCPRODCODE=&s_trackval=&s_referrer=&s_siteloc=&kbid=69919

26. Quoted in Schafer, 786.

27. Schafer proposes that Ann's bequest was motivated by her nieces' education at the Church Missionary Society School in Africa. More likely, it was Hectorina's influence, as she remembered the English missionaries that visited the Presbyterian Church and school in Philadelphia when the family lived there.

28 . Manucy, Vol.1, April 13, 3.

## Conclusion

1. Gordon, J. ed., *The New Statistical Accounts / by the ministers of the respective parishes, under the superintendence of a committee of the Society for the Benefit of the Sons and Daughters of the Clergy,* Ross and Cromarty, Vol. 14. Edinburgh. Blackwoods and Sons, 1845, p. 239. University of Edinburgh, University of Glasgow 1999. The Statistical Accounts online service. https://stataccscot.edina.ac.uk:443/link/nsa-vol14-p-239-contents-ross_and_cromarty-county-contnents

2. John M. Palmer, ed., *Bench and Bar in Illinois,* Historical and Reminiscent, 1899. https://archive.org/stream/benchbarofillino02palm/benchbarofillino02palm_djvu.txt 854.

## ILLUSTRATION CREDITS

1. Distaff and spindle: Pearson Scott Foresman donated to Wikimedia Foundation, adapted by author. https://commons.wikimedia.org/wiki/File:Distaff_%28PSF%29.png

2. Grant Fraser Mackenzie Tree by author.

3. Map of Philadelphia, 1807-18, adapted by author. Permission granted by Cornell Uiversity Press for use of map in Billy G. Smith, *The "Loweer Sort," Philadelphia's Laboring Class 1750-1800*, (Ithaca: Cornell University Press, 1990), 10. Drawing by Peter E. Daniels in 1982.

4. John Grant Advertisement, *Poulson's Daily Advertiser*, Philadelphia, Vol. XXXiX, Issue 10588 Octobe 1, 1810): 1. https://www.genealogybank.com/doc/newspapers/image/ v2%3A10380B4ABA623678%40GB3NEWS-10474D0E2BA2 243A%402382459-10474D0E3850F5BD%400-10474D0EF-B20AD64%40Advertisement?lname=grant&fname=john&-dateType=range&formDateFlex=exact&rgtoDate=1812&rgfrom-Date=1807

5. Ridgway Tree by author.

6. Gentleman John Ridgway, 1755-1845, Courtesy of Hagen Gelardin Center, Georgetown University Library, Washington D. C.

7. Sarah Ridgway Waln 1779-1872 Courtesy of Historic Walnford, Monmouth County, New Jersey Park System